REMARKS.

ON A

PAMPHLET,

ENTITLED

"THE PERPETUITY OF THE MORAL LAW."

BY

A. N. GROVES.

MADRAS:

J. B. PHAROAH.

ATHENÆUM PRESS—MOUNT ROAD.

———

MDCCCXL.

R. HOSIE, PRINTER.

PREFACE.

The following remarks on the "Perpetuity of the Moral Law" by a minister of the Establishment, I had hoped never to have had occasion to publish, thinking that it must be its own refutation; and I was the more confirmed in this opinion by the remark of a minister of the same Establishment concerning the work viz. that he considered it only remarkable for two things 1st the invidious use made of an unpopular name and 2nd the extraordinary errors of the Hebrew Criticism and of this in this country I think there was not a more competent Judge, but seeing that it is still publickly recommended as a full answer to the book it professes to review, I was induced by the wishes of those who had read the manuscript to publish it. But I have desired rather to make it a book that might give information on the subjects on which it treats than simply a reply to the attack.—And in fact the confusion and mistatement that pervades the work left me no choice but either of pursuing this plan or writing a large volume to prove how often the author had asserted what I never denied, and denied what I never asserted, how often he had confounded the Sinai covenant with the whole old Testament Scriptures, and the decalogue with the whole Sinai covenant and above all how often he had confounded the teaching of Our Lord to Jews[*] to whom alone he was

[*] "I am not sent save unto the lost sheep of the House of Israel." "It is not meet to take the childrens bread and to cast it to dogs." The command also to the disciples not to go into any City of the Samaritans, nor into the way of the Gentlies.

sent personally whilst the whole Jewish Law was in force, and the Apostles of the circumcision, with that teaching which was promulgated by the Spirit through Him who was emphatically called the apostle of the *uncircumcision*, though it seemed good to the whole assembly of Apostles and Elders and the Church at Jerusalem *with the Spirit* to lay down an ordinance constituting a difference which was recognised till the days of Constantine. Who pronounced also those observances declared *orderly in a Jew* namely *walking after the law of Moses and the customs*, to be subverting the souls of the Gentiles, and therefore they enjoined that they should observe no such things. I cannot believe this was intentional on the part of our author but arose out of the indistinct views, he had of the point at issue. The very title of the Pamphlet has no place, for I never denied the perpetuity of the Moral Law as existing in the Divine Mind, but that either the Decalogue or the whole Sinai covenant even, was a full development of it; and I confess it appears to me still a most arbitrary and unwarrantable assumption for any man to confine the term moral law to the Decalogue and thereby exclude the loving God with all your heart Deut. vi. 5 and your neighbour as your self Lev. xix. 18. the laws of kindness and pity to the poor; indeed let any one read the xviii. xix. and xx. Chapters of Lev. and ask himself if most of these instructions are not moral laws in the same sense as the Decalogue, see again those in Deut. xxvii. indeed unless our author has some peculiar definition of the term moral this limitation seems to me inexplicable. It must be borne in mind in the following pages that the term *law* is never used with reference to our justification but merely as a *rule of life* if therefore I use the term law of Christ, or those shall perish who obey not the Gospel of Our Lord Jesus Christ I mean the term simply as referring to a rule of life, and I believe our author would equally with myself reject both as that by an obedience to which we should be justified before God. His accusation is that if I take not the Decalogue I am without law, an antinomian, a lawless one; my object is to prove that those who walk after the manner and according to the precepts of Jesus and his Apostles not only are not lawless and have a rule of life, but one beyond all comparison more strict and extensive, more minute and heart searching than that which he proposes both for conviction of sin, and as a rule of God like righteousness.

A REPLY

TO THE

PERPETUITY OF THE MORAL LAW, &c.

In publishing the following remarks on the "Perpetuity of the Moral Law" I hope to be guided, not so much by the desire of self-vindication, as the establishment of truth. The quotations and criticisms it will be better to meet afterwards by proof, than by here merely stating my opinion of them. The way in which our author commences his work, the preface did not lead me to expect, for therein he expresses the following sentiment: "Let truth be ever regarded as sacred, even if held by the most abandoned. Let error be always exposed, even if held by the most pious." Yet he begins by seeking to prejudice the minds of his readers, by instituting an unfounded comparison between my views, and those of the Anabaptists of the 16th century. Now surely what was incumbent on him by his own principle, was not to have shewn that I held views in common with some other obnoxious individuals, but that we both held views in common contrary to scripture. Nothing is more easy than instituting comparisons; and Demetrius, the silver-smith at Ephesus, would have served my purpose quite as well as the Anabaptists did our author's, as illustrating at least thus much, that men, when they think their craft is in danger, that, whereby they get their livelihood, or respectability act very similarly in all ages, stirring up the people and making them think their religion is in danger, and although the greater part know not why they cry out, yet still they cry to keep their companions company, yet what Demetrius really had at heart, was the interests of himself and fellow craftsmen, and his real fear was not about religion and the image which fell down from Jupiter; but lest truth should so far prevail as that his trade might become no longer in request, had the new religion equally required silver shrines and had he an equal hope of living by making them as those of Diana, I feel assured, we should have heard nothing of Demetrius as the opponent of Paul or the advocate of the goddess Diana. What a parallel again might be drawn between the Romish and English establishments, accounting for the admiration bestowed by Pope Clement the 8th, on the ecclesiastical polity of Hooker, its grand advocate, and concerning which, James II. declared it was *one* of two books *that promoted his conversion to the church of Rome*, by shewing the extended similarity that exists between them, and leaving entirely out of sight those points in which they differ. When you are writing to expose particular defects, be they ever so numerous, you have nothing to do with the general character of the whole system to which they belong, but when the design is to leave an impression of a whole system by bringing it into comparison with another system, common honesty requires that the differences as well as agreements should be pointed out; if our Author had taken up point by point what he considered my errors and exposed them,

I should have felt (had he done it in a Christian spirit) that he was fully justified, but nothing can justify an odious association with any sect or party being attempted to be established when there is no agreement in those points which make them odious though there may be in others innocent perhaps or holy; in fact these are nothing better than polemical dishonesties that however common can never be justified, but on the contrary regarded as things deeply to be deplored as tending to obscure the questions at issue and embitter the spirit in which the enquiry professedly after truth is carried on.

ANABAPTISTS.

The *comparisons instituted by* the Author in the opening pages of his work, and from which he argues are the following *between my doctrines and those held by the Anabaptists and Mennonites:* but we will consider first the following quotation from his pamphlet, respecting the former of these sects.

He says, these people maintained, among others, the following points of doctrine: " That the church of Christ ought to be exempt from all sin—that all things ought to be in common among the faithful—that all usury, tithes, and tribute, ought to be entirely abolished—that the baptism of infants was an invention of the devil—that every Christian was invested with a power to preach the gospel: and, consequently, that the church stood in no need of ministers and pastors—that in the kingdom of Christ, civil magistrates were absolutely useless—and that God still continued to reveal his will to chosen persons by dreams and visions."

I will now consider these views seriatim. 1st as to *the Church being without all-sin* whatever she ought to be, I know she is not without the deepest guilt and sin, but if she ought not to be free from all sin will the author say what sins she ought to be defiled with, and if sin be absolutely necessary to her what does this mean that " God will not allow you to be tempted above that you are able," I always thought all and every sin was the Church's shame and iniquity, not her necessity. 2dly that *all things ought to be in common* among the faithful; this I never taught and never held*, though I have ever felt that such love should prevail that our abundance should supply the need of the poor so that if one member suffer all the members should suffer with it, and if one member rejoice all the members should rejoice with it. 3dly, as to *usury* I think it unlawful because against the common law of England as well as opposed to the whole spirit of the Gospel. As to *Tithes* though I would never demand them nor receive them and though I look on them as a mere badge of judaism yet since adopted by the state and because part of the law of the land I always paid them as any other tax, and never did or would sign even a petition against them, neither did I ever regard them as any *civil* hardship, though I believe them in the mode of their collection, payment, and application in nineteen cases out of twenty most opposed to the will of God and to the interests of Christs' kingdom. As to paying *tribute* I think I need hardly say that to ren-

---

* If a common stock is hereby meant, so that an individual surrendered his uncontrouled right of disposal to whom and how he pleased, amenable only to God.

der "tribute to whom tribute is due and custom to whom custom is due," is a precept I esteem binding on every Christian, and whilst remembering our Lord's words, render unto *Cæsar* the things that are *Cæsars*, and unto *God* the things that are *God's;* I could neither justify the robbery of Cæsar for a burnt offering to God, nor the robbing of God to pay tribute unto Cæsar. 4thly, as to *infant baptism being the invention of the Devil*, I would observe, that I do most fully believe, that this doctrine has no support from any precept or practice contained in scripture, and in this I am not singular; for Bishop Burnet, Dr. Wall, Luther, Zuinglius, Melancthon, Baxter, Calvin, Vetringa, Limborch, Bishop Sanderson, Bishop Stillingfleet, and a host of others, all fully allow the same, yet they were not Anabaptists. To those who hold tradition and inferential arguments this may not be sufficient, but to those who wish to stand only by what is written in the scriptures, it is conclusive against the practice.* As to *immer-*

---

* It is an interesting fact that in the year 596, Gregory the Great, of Rome, sent over Austin, an abbot, with about 40 monks, to convert the English. On his arrival, he found that he had been long preceded by the gospel of Christ, and that multitudes of persons had received it for ages. He labours to unite them with, in order to bring them under the authority of the Church of Rome, but in vain. At length he calls their ministers together, and proposed three things to them, to which, if they objected, the sword of war should be the penalty.

These he thus expressed :—" The 1st is, that ye keep Easter-day
" in the form and time as it is ordained; the 2d, that ye give
" Christendome (or baptism) to children; and the 3d, that ye
" preach unto the Angles the word of God, as I have exhorted
" you." To these the British firmly objected, and, painful to add, suffered the threatened fate.

sion instead of sprinkling: Whitby says "It was a practice "religiously observed *by all Christians* for 13 centuries, "and approved of by our Church, and the change of "it into sprinkling without any allowance from the "author of this institution, being that which the Romanist uses to justify his refusal of the Cup to the "laity, it were to be wished the custom were to be "again of general use." But at all events, Anabaptists sprinkled and did not immerse, and therefore in this evident departure from scripture and antiquity, their resemblance is to be found with our Author, and not with us. 5thly, That *every Christian was invested with the power to preach the Gospel.* I utterly deny ever having either held or stated any such doctrine, on the contrary, I think comparatively few have the power, what I said was that those who have the power given them of the Holy Ghost, enabling them to minister, have a right to minister, nay, are bound to minister; and woe be to them if they do not, and that man has neither power nor right given him of God to make a minister, nor hinder one; indeed the Holy Ghost alone can give the right, and we are to prove a man's pretension to the right by his spiritual ability, doctrine and life, not by the laying on of hands. 6thly, *As to Pastors*, whilst I contend, that none are pastors, or elegible to the office who do not answer to the character, and are not qualified by the Holy Ghost, in the manner, described by Paul in Timothy and Titus. I assert and ever have that pastors are essential to all divine rule, and that as such, they are to be obeyed, but both nature itself as well as scripture teaches me that youths of 24, never can answer the scripture requirements. You might as well make women teachers of men, as youths, rulers of their elders, they are equally repugnant to God's word, and all right moral feeling. 7thly, That in the kingdom of Christ *civil magistrates* were absolutely useless. Had the Anabaptists meant that to those who walk like Jesus, fulfilling the will of the Father, loving their neighbour as themselves, and treating their enemies as God does his in this dispensation, returning them good for evil, and loving their Heavenly Father with all their hearts and souls, and strength, needed not the civil magistrate for themselves; I would quite concur, for I cannot conceive what need any Church of Christ, which is so walking, has of civil magistrates, all whose institutions are designed to punish the unruly and wicked. Rom. xiii: 3. But as they regarded civil magistracy as no longer essential to the ordering the affairs of this world, and as such not to be obeyed, but resisted, they directly opposed that scripture which declares that the powers that be are ordained of God and to be prayed for as such, and submitted to in all those matters over which they have authority, and even should they lay their hands on that which is God's they are to be resisted, not by rebellion, but by submissive endurance. But when our author, condemns us for declining the sword altogether, whether that of war or of the civil magistrate as a weapon, unlawful for the saint to use in this dispensation, by what tortuous ingenuity he satisfied his own mind as to the reality of the parallelism he institutes, I am at a loss to conceive. 8thly, That *God still continues to reveal his will to chosen persons by dreams and visions;* to this, all I can say is, that if it be so as long as any one who dreams or sees a vision confines the application of it to his own profit, and does not force it upon the Church, I have nothing to say, one way or the other, and therefore, can neither affirm or deny the statement, yet of course with this reserve, that they never contain any thing contrary to the written word, in which case they are of course to be rejected entirely.

I therefore dismiss the charge of union in principle or feeling with the Anabaptists, as one of pure misrepresentation, and as such to be submitted to by the Christian who knows that his Lord has said " blessed " are ye when men shall revile you and persecute you, " and speak *all manner of evil against you falsely for " my sake.*" Our Lord was called Beelzebub, a breaker of God's laws, and a profaner of the Sabbath, by his own people the Jews, because he opposed their false and foolish traditions and their subversions of his Father's will, and " if they called the master of the " house Beelzebub, how much more they of the house- " hold."

MENNONITES.

The Author having finished his account of the views and practices of the Anabaptists institutes another comparison between my opinions and those of the Mennonites, in reference to which, he makes the following extract from Mosheim's Ecclesiastical history.

" The religious opinions which still distinguish the Mennonites from all other Christian communities, flow directly from the ancient doctrine of the Anabaptists concerning the nature of the Church. It is in consequence of this doctrine, that they admit none to the sacrament of baptism, but persons that are come to the full use of their reason; because infants are incapable of binding themselves by a solemn vow to a holy life ; and it is altogether uncertain, whether or no, in maturer years, they will be saints or sinners. It is in consequence of the same doctrine, that they neither admit civil rulers into their communion, nor allow any one of their members to perform the functions of magistracy; for where there are no malefactors, magistrates are useless. Hence do they pretend also to deny the lawfulness of repelling force by force, and consider war in all its shapes as unchristian and unjust, for as those who are perfectly holy can neither be provoked by injuries, nor commit them, they do not stand in need of the force of arms, either for the purposes of resentment or defence. It is still the same principle that excites in them the utmost aversion to the execution of justice, and more especially to capital punishments; since according to this principle, there are no transgressions or crimes in the kingdom of Christ, and consequently no occasion for the arm of the judge. They allege, that Christ had promulgated A NEW LAW OF LIFE, far more perfect than that which had been delivered by Moses and the prophets: and they excluded from their communion all such as deviated, in the least from the most rigorous rules of simplicity and gravity in their looks, their gesture, their clothing, and their table: all those desires which surpassed the dictates of mere necessity."

As to the comparison instituted above, between my opinions and those of the Mennonites, though in many respects they differ, yet those quoted are not wholly dissimilar, except that I feel, there is no warrant from scripture for declining church fellowship with any on account of the exercise of magistracy or arms, so much even as for laying up money, and therefore feel that nothing but evil could result from forcing such a yoke on the consciences of others. But however, this may be, I cannot but agree with the author of the following remarks in the Encyclopædia Britannica as to the origin of this sect in preference to the more prejudiced statement of Dr. Mosheim as quoted above from our Authors pamphlet. The remarks are as follows :—

"It must be observed, that the Baptists and Mennonites of England and Holland, are to be considered in a very different light from the enthusiasts (the Ana-Baptists) we have been describing; and *it appears equally uncandid and invidious, to trace up their distinguishing sentiment, as some of their adversaries have done, to those obnoxious characters*, and there to stop, in order, as it were, to associate with it the ideas of turbulence and fanaticism, with which it certainly has no natural connexion."

"They appear supported by history in considering themselves the descendants of the Waldenses,* who were so grievously oppressed and persecuted by the despotic heads of the Romish monarchy; and they profess an equal aversion to all *principles of rebellion on* one hand, and to all *suggestions of fanaticism on the other*."

From the above, as well as from what follows, it is evident that all the distinguishing views of the Mennonites are traceable up to the very times of the Apostles. Tatian in the second century, thus describes the moral character of the Christians of his day "I wish not

---

* Theodore Beza: speaking of these people says "as for the 'Waldenses, I may be permitted to call them the very seed of "the primitive church," and Rienerius Saccho, who had been connected with the Waldenses, above 17 years, and afterwards apostatized and became an inquisitor, and most cruel persecutor of this people, testifies, "that the Waldenses flourished five hundred years before the appearance of Peter Waldo;" that is, before A. D. 1160, which refers their history back to A. D. 660.

" to reign, I wish not to be rich, I *avoid military office*; I abhor fornication."* Athenagoras when pointing out to the emperors the real character of christianity, after declaring the heathen, made "their profession a mere " flourish of words and not a rule of practice:" says "but " among us you may find illiterate persons, and arti- " sans, and old women, who, if they cannot show the " benefits resulting from their profession by their " words, show it by practice. For they do not com- " mit words to memory, but show forth good deeds: " *when struck, they strike not again—when robbed,* " *they have not recourse to the law*—they give to those " who ask—and love their neighbours as themselves."*— As to the question of a NEW LAW, I do not here argue the point, as it will be after fully treated; but merely quote one passage to prove that this doctrine owed not its origin to the Anabaptists or Mennonites. Tertullian in his Tract adversus Judæos " says it is certain " that Jesus, whom we affirm to be *the promised law-* " *giver, has promulgated a* NEW LAW." (5)

PREMILLENIAL ADVENT.

Having now made the above remarks on our Authors comparison between my doctrines and those of the Anabaptists and Mennonites, there is another important point that still remains, to be alluded to and that is the doctrine of the premillenial advent of our Saviour (see p. 8) and which it seems he likewise

* See the Bishop of Lincoln's account of the writings of Justin Martyr p. 210.
* Ibid. p. 213
(5) See the Bp. of Bristol's Ecc. Hist. p. 466.

imagines " came upon the stage at or about the time " of the Reformation and was adopted by the Anabap- " tists of Germany with such fearful results." As to the Anabaptists, their error consisted not in believing that there would be a millenium, the 5th Monarchy of Daniel which was to destroy its predecessors; but in that they thought the time for the setting up of the kingdom was then come, and that rebellion against the powers that be, and various abominations in private life were the means and harbingers to usher in such a time of blessedness to the Church in particular, and to the world at large. But does our author need to be informed, that a very large body, both of the Ministers and members of his own establishment (and that blessed be God a rapidly increasing body) hold views similar to mine as to the grand truth of a premillenial advent, and I will leave them to answer, whether they learnt it from the rebels of Munster. This subject is however of such importance in leading the Church to a right view of her present position in the world that I shall not dismiss it here (as I might do as far as any thing in the " Perpetuity" is affected by the question) (6) but seek as briefly as possible to shew, 1st that with scarce an exception all the orthodox members of the Church in the first, second, and third centuries held

(6) I feel it also the more necessary to make a few remarks on this subject as I know a pamphlet in support of Antimillenarianism has lately been circulated and I would here strongly recommend to all interested in the enquiry a valuable little work entitled " Elements of prophetic interpretation" by the Rev. J. W. Brooks.

the second coming of our Saviour to be an event that should take place previous to, and usher in the thousand years of glory and blessedness. 2ndly, that the rise of the Antimillenarian doctrine was not amongst the orthodox but the heretics, and which became general only with the general corruption of Christianity at the time of Constantine and increased in universality with the increasing darkness of the middle ages and 3rdly, I shall endeavour to shew what were the reasons that made the Antimillenarian doctrine so acceptable to the Church at the time when it first began to gain the ascendancy.

1st. As to the antiquity and universality of the belief in the doctrine of a premillenial advent of our Saviour, among the orthodox of the primitive Church, without going to the Scriptures (for it might be easily proved to have been the only doctrine preached by our Saviour and his Apostles, and the only one received by their converts as has been abundantly shewn by many writers on the subject) I would in the first place quote the following striking passage from Justin Martyr, who says, in his Dialogue with Trypho " I, and all Christians who are orthodox in all things
" (ορθονωμενες κατα παντα) are acquainted with the
" resurrection of the body and the thousand years reign
" in Jerusalem that shall be re-edified, adorned and
" enlarged as the prophets Ezekial, Isaiah, and others
" declare................Moreover a certain man
" among us whose name is John, being one of the 12
" Apostles of Christ in that revelation that was shown
" unto him prophesied, that those who believe in our

"Christ shall fulfil a thousand years at Jerusalem; and after that shall be the general, and in a word the everlasting resurrection, and last judgment of all." But he is not the only writer of the Church in the first four centuries who mentions his belief in the doctrine Barnabas, Papias, Polycarp, Irenæus, Tertullian, Lactantius, Epiphanius, Paulinus bishop of Antioch, Gregory of Nyssa, and many others have done the same; (7) and Jerome who was himself a warm opponent to the doctrine, says "*he durst not condemn the doctrine because many ecclesiastical persons and martyrs affirmed the same.*" (8) But besides all the abundant testimony which exists from the above mentioned and other writers of those times to the correctness of my statement modern historians bear testimony to the same. Mosheim himself an evident opponent of the doctrine in his account of the 3d century, after stating that "the controversy concerning the millenium or reign of a thousand years" was among the controversies that divided the Christians during that century says "long before this period an opinion had prevailed that Christ was to come and reign a thousand years among men before the entire and final dissolution of the world. This opinion which *had hitherto met with no opposition*, was variously interpreted by different persons, nor did all promise themselves the same kind of enjoyments in that future and

(7) For quotations from most of the above writers I would refer my readers to the 3d Chap. of Mr. Brooks' work on prophecy before mentioned.

(8) See Jerome on Jeremiah, xix.

" glorious kingdom; but in this century, its credit *be-*
" *gan to decline* principally through the influence and
" authority of Origen who opposed it with the greatest
" warmth, *because it was incompatible with some of*
" *his favorite sentiments*" and it is not amiss here to
observe that upon the same grounds he was led to
question the canonical authority of the book of Revelations itself as many others holding his sentiments
have done. The learned Dodwell observes " the pri-
" mitive Christians believed that the first resurrection
" of their bodies would take place in the kingdom of
" the millenium. And as they considered that resur-
" rection to be peculiar to the just, so they conceived the
" martyrs would enjoy the principal share of its glory.
" Since these opinions were entertained, it is impossi-
" ble to say how many were inflamed with the desire
" of martyrdom." (9) There is however one quotation more that I would desire to make upon the subject,
and that is from the pen of one who was a very diligent observer of the affairs of the christians though an
unfriendly one; it is as follows :—" The ancient chris-
" tians were animated by a Contempt for their present
" existence and by a just confidence of immortality, of
" which *the doubtful but imperfect faith of modern*
" *ages* cannot give us any adequate notion. It was

---

(9) Jam in millennii regno primam fore resurrectionem corporum crediderunt primævi Christiani. Et ut justorum propriam eam crediderunt resurrectionem, ita martyrum in ea portionem longe esse præcipuam. Hæc cum ita crederentur, dici nequit quantum martyres illius ætatis martyrii studio inflammarint Dodwelli Dissert. Cyprian. xii. De Martyrum fortitudine, sect. 20, 21.

"universally believed, that the end of the world and
"the kingdom of Heaven, were at hand. The near
"approach of this wonderful event had been predicted
"by the apostles; the tradition of it was preserved by
"their earliest disciples, and those who understood in
"their literal sense the discourses of Christ himself,
"were obliged to expect the second and glorious com-
"ing of the Son of man in the clouds, before that ge-
"neration was totally extinguished, which had beheld
"his humble condition upon earth, and which might
"still be witness of the calamities of the Jews under
"Vespasian or Adrian. The revolution of seventeen
"centuries has instructed us not to press too closely
"the mysterious language of prophecy and revelation;
"but as long as, for wise purposes, this error was per-
"mitted to subsist in the church, *it was productive of
"the most salutary effects on the faith and practice of
"Christians*, (10) who lived in the awful expectation of
"that moment when the globe itself, and all the vari-
"ous races of mankind, should tremble at the appear-
"ance of their divine judge. The ancient and popu-
"lar doctrine of the millennium was intimately con-
"nected with the second coming of Christ. As the
"works of the creation had been finished in six days,
"their duration in their present state, according to a

(10) It does strike the mind with surprise to see an infidel so clearly tracing the practical results of this most sustaining doctrine to which even believers in this day blinded by prejudice deny any practical consequences at all. All I can say is if it lead not *now* to deeply practical results, it must be from what Gibbon calls " the " doubtful and imperfect faith of modern ages."

" tradition which was attributed to the prophet Elijah,
" was fixed to six thousand years (11.)

" By the same analogy it was inferred, that this
" long period of labour and contention, which was
" now almost elapsed, would be succeeded by *a
" joyful Sabbath of a thousand years;* and *that
" Christ, with the triumphant band of the Saints
" and the elect who had escaped death, or who
" had been miraculously revived, would reign
" upon earth till the time appointed for the last
" and general resurrection.* The assurance of such a
" millennium, was carefully inculcated by a succession
" of fathers from Justin Martyr and Irenæus, who
" conversed with the immediate disciples of the apos-
" tles, down to Lactantius, who was preceptor to the
" son of Constantine. *Though it might not be uni-
" versally received, it appears to have been the reign-
" ing sentiment of the orthodox believers;* and it seems
" so well adapted to the desires and apprehensions of
" mankind, that it must have contributed in a very
" considerable degree, to the progress of the Chris-
" tian faith. But *when* the edifice of the Church was
" almost completed, the temporary support was laid
" aside. The doctrine of Christ's reign upon earth,
" was at first treated as a profound allegory, was con-
" sidered by degrees as a doubtful and useless opinion,

(11) The primitive Church of Antioch computed almost 6000 years from the creation of the world to the birth of Christ. Africanus Lactantius and the Greek Church have reduced that number to 5500, and Eusebius has contented himself with 5,200. These calculations were founded on the Septuagint, which was universally received during the first six centuries.

"and was at length rejected as the absurd invention
"of heresy and fanaticism. A mysterious prophecy,
"which still forms a part of the sacred canon, but
"which was thought to favour the exploded senti-
"ment, has very narrowly escaped the proscription of
"the Church. Whilst the happiness and glory of a
"temporal reign were promised to the disciples of
"Christ, the most dreadful calamities were denounc-
"ed against an unbelieving world. The edification
"of the New Jerusalem was to advance by equal steps
"with the destruction of the mystic Babylon; and as
"long as the emperors who reigned before Constan-
"tine persisted in the profession of idolatry, the
"epithet of Babylon was applied to the city and to
"the empire of Rome. A regular series was prepar-
"ed of all the moral and physical evils which can af-
"flict a flourishing nation; intestine discord, and the
"invasion of the fiercest barbarians from the un-
"known regions of the North; pestilence and famine,
"comets and eclipses, earthquakes and inundations.
"All these were only so many preparatory and alarm-
"ing signs of the great catastrophe of Rome, when
"the country of the Scipios and Cæsars should be
"consumed by a flame from Heaven, and the city of
"the seven hills, with her palaces, her temples, and
"her triumphal arches, should be buried in a vast
"lake of fire and brimstone." (13) Now in the fore-
going quotation there is, although accompanied with
the profane sneer and ungodly scepticism of infidelity
as clear a statement of the extent and manner in which

(13) See Gibbon's Roman Empire, Vol. 1 p. 277.

the doctrine of a millennium was received in the Church up to the time of Constantine, as could possibly be desired for (as we have seen above) that " though it might *not be universally received* it appears " to have been *the reigning sentiment of the orthodox* " *believers.*" (14)

And this testimony is the more valuable as it comes from one who could have had no pre-conceived religious views to bias his judgment. By all the preceding, I trust I have proved to the satisfaction of every unprejudiced mind, that the doctrine of the premillenial advent of our Lord, was no more new in the 16th century than now; but that it was the almost universal belief of all the orthodox in the primitive Church! We now come to the next point, viz.:

2dly. That the rise of the Antimillenarian doctrine was not among the orthodox, but the heretics. The first germ of this evil and pernicious doctrine, we find in Paul's Epistle to Timothy where he is warning him to avoid Hymenæus and Philetus " who concerning the faith had erred " saying that *the* resurrection " (την αναστασιν) had passed already" (2 Tim: 2. 16—18) which was equivalent to saying that there

---

(14) In reference to the universality of the belief in the doctrine of a premillenial advent, the learned Mede observes as follows : " If we except the primary and fundamental articles of our " faith, perhaps all antiquity does not furnish us with a stronger " testimony than this to the truth of any christian doctrine. What " a presumptive argument have we here in favor of its being " Apostolical, in that it was received by *all orthodox men* at a time " so near the apostles, when it is highly credible, that many were " then living, who heard the truth from their mouths."

would be no first resurrection (15) which it must ever be borne in mind, was, in the minds of the primitive christians intimately connected with and preceding the thousand years reign over (επι) the earth, and to which their fondest hopes were directed. The denial of this most important doctrine gave rise to the denial of many others connected with it, as is evident from the following quotation from Justin Martyr, which stands just before a quotation from his dialogue with Trypho previously alluded to. He says " I have be-
" fore confessed to thee that *I and many others are of*
" *this opinion* [namely; that Jerusalem shall be rebuilt
" and the saints enjoy a happy life on earth with Christ]
" so that we hold it to be thoroughly proved that it
" will come to pass. But I have also signified unto
" thee on the other hand, that *many even those of the*
" *race of christians, who follow not godly and pure*
" *doctrine, do not acknowledge it.* For I have de-
" monstrated to thee that *these are indeed called*
" *christians; but are atheists and impious heretics,*
" *who altogether teach blasphemous atheistical and*
" *unsound things.*" (16) From which we learn that

(15) In proof that the resurrection here alluded to is not the general resurrection, but the first resurrection. See a tract entitled "the heresy of Hymenæus and Philetus, concerning the first resurrection" by James A Begg.

(16) It is necessary to remark here on the above quotation, that in the printed copies of Justin Martyr, the word *not*, in the sentence "not godly and pure" is wanting and although omitted in most of the manuscripts extant in the 17th century, is *not so in all*. The internal evidence is however so overwhelmingly strong for the word " *not*" having formed part of the original text, that its being comitted by every MS. would scarce be a sufficient warrant for its omission, for observe the very next sentence is "*for I have before*
" *demonstrated to thee that* THESE *are indeed called christians but*

in the days of Justin Martyr it was considered unorthodox to hold any doctrine, which should in any way militate against the millennium, or any of those glorious events so closely connected with it. These unscriptural and heretical views were, however, with many others of a similar nature adopted by Origen, concerning whom I cannot better speak, than in the words of Milner, who says, that " no man, not altoge-
" ther unsound and hypocritical ever *injured the*
" *church of Christ, more than Origen did*. From the
" fanciful mode of allegory *introduced by him*, and un-
" controlled by scriptural rule and order, there arose
" a vitiated method of commenting on the sacred
" pages.........A thick mist for ages pervaded the
" christian, world supported and strengthened by his
" allegorical manner of interpretation. The learned
" alone were considered as guides implicitly to be fol-
" lowed; and the vulgar, when *the literal sense* was
" hissed off the stage, had nothing to do, but to follow
" their authority, wherever it might lead them." (17)
The like testimony is given by Mosheim, Luther and others respecting this in other respects learned and good man. The evil however stopped not here, although

"*are really atheists, &c.*" which, if the word "*not*" be omitted, would apply to the followers of "*godly and pure* doctrine." The cause of its being expunged from some of the original MSS. is evident as by its retention the Romanists would have had an insurmountable traditionary evidence of the truth of those views of the millennium, which from sinister motives, they had been constrained to reject. See the quotation and some critical remarks on it in " Brooks on prophecy." p 63.

(17) See Milner's church History, vol. 1. p. 469.

opposed by the majority (18) it was received by many with various modifications, and was subsequently adopted by Jerome, who became its strenuous supporter, as also by the historian Eusebius who lived in the reign of Constantine, but, who besides, being unorthodox (for he was tainted with the Arian heresy) also endeavoured to insinuate that the Apocalypse was the work of Cerinthus the Ebionite, because he found it opposed to his system. From this period the millenial reign, which had been regarded by some of the ancient heretics, as well as Origen and his followers, either as an unscriptural doctrine, or " a profound allegory" began more and more generally to be considered " as a " doubtful and useless opinion, and was at length re-" jected as the absurd invention of heresy and fana-" ticism" by the majority of the professing church, during the darkest ages of Popery. Thus we have traced this anti-millenarian doctrine from its first rise as the heretical doctrine of a few " athiests and heretics," to its gradually being received by some whose principles of allegorizing away the sacred scriptures became as Mosheim affirms " the secure retreat for all sorts of " errors which a wild and irregular imagination could bring forth." (19) And finally, to its becoming the prevailing (for it was never the *only*) tenet of the professing church. We now come to the last point, viz.

3rdly. As to the reason that made the Antimillenarian doctrine, so acceptable to the church at the time when it first began to gain the ascendancy. As long as the Church of Christ, generally stood in its true po-

(18) Nepos, a pious and learned Bishop of Egypt, wrote a book expressly against this system of interpretation, entitled " The Reprehensions of the Allegorizers."

(19) See Mosheim's Ecc. Hist III. cent.

sition of witness against the world, it had no inducement to suppress or hide from itself the down-fall and ruin of that power, by which it felt oppressed, impoverished and persecuted, and so long as all those peculiar doctrines of poverty, passive obedience, non-resistance of evil, prevailed, the scripture doctrine of the speedy advent of Christ to establish his millenial kingdom, and to bring down that which was lofty and exalt that which was abased, was the solace and joy of the church. But no sooner had things so changed, that the outcast trampled religion became seated professedly on the throne of the Cæsars, than the whole face of things changed; with the growing prosperity in external things, the desire of the advent of the Son of God to judge the nations became all but extinct and this arose from the natural tendency there is in prosperity to deaden the longing for the coming of Christ even in the saints; but the chief source of this forgetfulness lay not here, for no sooner had Constantine (the true Jeroboam of the christian church) conceived like his predecessor the design of making a political use of God's religion, by connecting it with the State, modifying its character, and placing himself at its head than every species and extent of corruption came in with it. The smiles and patronage of the monarch increased beyond conception, the multitudes of professors and proved allurements to ambition and pride that soon brought in a set of men, whose enormous depravity and corruption paved the way for Mahomedanism and Popery, the two daughters of this union the Sodom and Samaria of the christian church. Let any man unbiased by prejudice, ask himself, what possible acceptance the doctrine of the premillenial advent of the Son of God could have, which threatened only to visit upon the Roman Empire and its rulers the vengeance predicted, to bring all its deeds of darkness to light and dash it in pieces like a potter's vessel? as well might you expect the 1st advent of Jesus, as King of the Jews would have been acceptable to Herod, as this doctrine of his 2d advent to Constantine and his successors. These were doctrines unpalatable to all in whose hands patronage and power in the professing church was now lodged; nor will these doctrines ever again revive in power, but in proportion as we are able to say with Paul "the world is crucified unto me, and I unto the world;" it may so revive as to answer the purpose of a well lightened and carpeted drawing-room lecture, as a pretty theory, but will never be entered into and desired, but as by following Christ in all the self-devoted consecration of his character we so really renounce the world, the flesh and the devil, as to look on all that is in it, the "lust of the flesh, the lust of the eye, and the pride of life," as "not of the Father, but of the world."

CHURCH CANONS.

Our author has also called the attention of his readers to a little collection of texts of scripture, affording rules to guide the saints of God in various matters of a public and private nature, called Church canons. To these remarks I would simply say, I had nothing to do either with the compiling or printing of the tract, nor till the arrival of the author's book, had I read it or *circulated* it, but since I have, my conviction is, that it is a valuable little collection as far as it goes, not perfect, nor pretending to be so, but confessedly the contrary. These canons were never designed as our author supposes for any particular church or churches even, much less as canons for the universal church, farther than they convey to any individual reading them the mind of Christ nor do they assume any higher authority as to their arrangement than Chalmers' scripture references, or Clarke's scripture promises: and even had they assumed more than they do, seeing they are only from the word of the living God, the "presumption or arrogance" would not have been half as "insufferable" as the canons and ecclesiastical constitution of his own establishment, with all its *ipso facto* excommunications for the rejection of canons that have not for the *most part* a trace of scripture to rest on; but which in their whole character are much better suited to the mystic Babylon than a church of Christ. This little collection was made merely to shew, that the great Head of the Church had become himself the canonist on those subjects in this collection introduced, and in others, possibly more numerous not introduced. I think one addition the author proposes as to baptism most necessary, and should a second edition be published, which I hear, is now likely to be the case, I hope to see it in and many others; but that *believers* ought to be immersed, which is all that scripture canons teach, never could have been intentionally omitted by one who held and practised it, as the compiler of those texts had done. If it had been to escape a recording of texts that supported the sprinkling of infants, or sponsors, or confirmation, or the sabbath, then indeed there might have been some ground for the unlovely manner in which quite unnecessarily this subject has been by the author mixed up with one, with which it had nothing to do. As to the omission of any canon relative to the observance of the Lord's day, the compiler seems to have done all that a compiler could, seeing that there was no separate precept concerning this observance as a separate duty, distinct from those duties in connection with which, and for the sake of which apparently the Holy Ghost had mentioned it at all; namely, in connection with some of the things that were to be done on it, as commemorating the death of Christ, giving to the poor, &c., under which heads therefore all the texts will be found that relate to the Lord's day, so far therefore the canonist and the Holy scriptures stand together for whilst the Holy Spirit gives 20 direct canons about filthy lucre, it gives not one direct and express canon about the necessity of observing the Lord's day. What our author means to imply by his quotation from the Latin poet:

"O cives cives! quærenda pecunia primum est
Virtus post nummos."

I know not, but this I know, that many of those to whom he applies it, instead of putting money in the first place, and virtue in the second, have lost more, *to keep a conscience* of all that this world values than most have gained *who have sold theirs*.

LIBERTY OF MINISTRY.

The author has also quite misrepresented my statement in the liberty of ministry. I feel assured, that the position of the churches will soon bring them as to their present forms into a deadly struggle with the world growing daily more infidel, who will resume, or try for it, those earthly things they think the folly of their forefathers gave away; my desire was to see the Dove the undefiled one of Christ (see Canticles) which is but one in establishments or out of them, rise above these waves of discord, and tell to the Legislators of the earth, with regard to Cæsar's things, give command, and we will obey and relinquish to the last mite, but of the things of God intrusted to us by our Head and King, not one jot or one tittle will we yield, till He come whose right it is; I think this would have been the true place of dignity and of safety, but mixed up with the world and fostered as she feels herself by secular power, I have little hope for her safety; but through such a fire as shall take away her dross and tin. But surely I am not singular, let our author read the following observations which being in the church of Ireland Magazine may have additional weight with many. I think it is in the number for January 1836.

"There is not an educated individual in the British empire, who is not aware that the Established Church is placed at this juncture in an extraordinary position; its property, its patronage, its discipline; its rites, and ceremonies subject to the control of persons composing His Majesty's Government, who may be not only indifferent to its welfare, but actually hostile to its very existence." And with this "Popish prelates taunt her, whilst Dissenters cast it in her teeth, while radicals and infidels prophesy her ruin and rejoice over it." Where is then her help not in the clergy who are so "impoverished" "distracted and divided" to whom then does she turn? to her strong tower the Lord of Hosts? no, but "our eyes we turn to the laity to save their church—the church

"which belongs to them and their children,—the
"church which if not purified and reformed from the
"*monstrous abuse of parlimentary supremacy, &c.*"
Again the writer says, the Established Church is, "sub-
"servient to a ministry that may be to-day under Tory,
"to-morrow under Whig, the next day under Popish,
"and the next under Radical influence. And if our
"Bishops, possessing *seven eighths* of the parochial
"patronage, are to come forth with their lawn vest-
"ments cast over them by such conflicting and vary-
"ing hands, verily our Church will become a fit re-
"presentation of Babel; and the very confusion of
"hearts and tongues that must ensue, will not only
"frustrate edification, but cause a sure dispersion." I
never said nor meant to say that ministers of Christ
whether in establishments or out of them were vultures,
but applied this to those who were seeking to feast
themselves upon the church's secularities. But I did
say, that every institution in proportion as it presents
motives to worldly ambition in the way of rank, wealth
or official influence allures exactly in proportion as
they exist, those whose proper food and glory they are,
not that there is not a blessed remnant, the Lord be
praised, in most establishments that I have seen, in the
Greek, the Roman Catholic, and abundantly more in
others, but this is not in consequence of the desires
of the flesh, the desires of the eye, and the pride of
life connected with them, but notwithstanding these.
The wickedness and departure from God of Israel
did not prevent 7000 loyal ones remaining, neither in
our Lord's time did the general apostacy of priests and
people prevent there being still a faithful remnant

though the mass had by their traditions made void the law of God, and so now there is a remnant according to the election of Grace. And if I have expressed myself in any place so as to seem to include all Ministers of the Word, in establishments, or any systems out of them; I would express my deep regret for having apparently so done, for it never was in my thoughts. I only meant to imply *those who made it a profession to live or rise by in the world*, to which I believe there is in all systems, especially protestant ones, a multitude of most honorable exceptions, and I fully recognise such as Ministers of Christ if they have the Lord's credentials, namely, ability to minister given of Him, notwithstanding all that appears to me futile in their exclusive pretensions, as well as irregular and false in their manner of entrance, and ground of confidence in their divine appointment. They have a divine appointment and without it no man can minister acceptably to God; but it lies not in ought that man can give or take away, but simply in the calling and qualifying of the Holy Ghost, without these no man is a minister of God, let man do what he can, and with these any man is, let man refuse what he will. Satan's minister I only applied to those who were by secular advantages drawn into the place of christian ministry, whether in establishments, or out of them, wherever or whoever they might be and really did Satan's work. The placing of secularities in the position of carrion and those who serve for them in that of vultures, has, as might be naturally expected given great offense to those who felt themselves affected by the comparison; but if the terms *vulture carrion*, and

foul are so offensive, would the scripture terms *eagle*, *carcase* and *filthy* be more acceptable? if I thought so I would willingly substitute them. I had no intention of applying the above terms to any individuals, but those who resembled the shepherds of Israel described by Isaiah, when he says " His watchmen are blind;
" they are all ignorant, they are all *dumb dogs*, they
" cannot bark; sleeping, lying down, loving to slum-
" ber. Yea, they are *greedy dogs which can never*
" *have enough*, and they are shepherds that cannot
" understand, they *all look to their own way, every*
" *one for his gain from his quarter.*" ch. lvi. 10, 11. (20.)

If it be said that the expressions are too weighty for the evil, I confess, I think otherwise. But if the Lord said to the luke-warm Laodiceans I will *spew* you out of my mouth, I feel no terms can be too hard for this corrupting, degrading root of all evil.

BISHOPS, PRIESTS AND DEACONS.

There are moments when my heart would lead me to say more than as a christian I feel I ought when I see our author stating that I represent the name *bishops, priests and deacons*, as names invented by Satan; it is an unworthy calumny, that has no design, but to

(20.) Our author in his indignation at the application of the above expressions calls them "low scurrilities and vulgar abuse" but surely they are no more so then the expressions made use of by God himself in the mouth of his Holy prophets; but further I have very respectable authority for the use of these terms in Blair, who in his grave, when speaking of the beauty fallen into its jaws says:
" For this was all thy caution
" For this thy painful labours at the glass
" T' improve these charms and keep them in repair
" For which the spoiler thanks thee not. *Foul feeder!*
" *Coarse fare* and *carrion* please thee full as well
" And leave as keen a relish on the sense."

excite prejudice. In the passage in my tract, page 62, there is not one expression of objection to the term *bishop*, and the terms *priest* or *deacon* are never referred to. But not only does not this passage give the shadow of a ground for such a charge but it is contrary to the whole tenor of the work, as the quotations in the subjoined note abundantly prove. (21) That I have an objection that the above and *every other term* connected with Church matters, should be retained in the original language

(21) In page 30, there is the following passage "but while I "hold, it is by Christ's appointment alone that any one becomes a "minister of Christ, absolutely, or an apostle, or a prophet, yet I "fully admit that to constitute a man bishop, (a word which im- "plies union with a special flock) human authority is needed; that "is no man can with good sense" (attempt to force himself into the position of bishop over a particular flock) " assume to be bishop "over a particular flock if he have not at least the good-will and con- "sent of that flock" (he must retire before the rebellion of the flock as Christ did, though King before the rebellion of his people;) and "similarly, the deacon's office can be assumed by none without "the approbation of those whose money he is about to dispose of. "But this leaves my assertion untouched that no human authority "is needed to confer the abstract right to teach or preach or ad- "minister the Sacraments," (or rule) Again page 31, "If I be "asked how it came to pass that Church officers so soon gained "rank and were constituted into an order? I reply first, because "the respect which is naturally and fitly given to *elders*, especially "to those who *rule* well, soon accumulates, until an inherent dig- "nity is vested in the individuals, and a hierarchy, results which "is to the Church what an aristocracy is in a nation." Again, re- "member I do not say a labourer is not worthy of his hire. He is "most richly worthy; and woe be to that Church which disregards "the claim. If also a pastor be worth having, he is worth paying, "and whenever there is much spiritual work to be done, it is bad "economy to let much of his valuable time be employed in la- "bouring for his earthly sustenance. But these considerations "are not such as he is to urge on them, but which they are to "urge on him; and I would have the minister of Christ infinitely

in any translation of the Bible is most true, as I believe it has been universally in some way or other at the expense of truth, the primary or simple scriptural idea has been lost sight of, and a secondary and false one substituted in its stead, which has owed its origin to a period when the exaltation of those, who were called the clergy, was the main design, not the exaltation of Jesus. James the First knew too well, the magic power of these unknown terms, with the majority, to allow Tindal's translation of them to stand, as it would have tended to remove that unholy awe founded on ignorance, which the retention of these words has been so instrumental in fostering. Had those, called apostles, been designated *messengers*, and those sent forth by Christ the *messengers of Christ* ($\alpha\pi o\sigma\tau o\lambda o\iota\ \tau o\upsilon\kappa\upsilon\rho\iota o\upsilon$) in contradistinction to the *messengers of the Churches* ($\alpha\pi o\sigma\tau o\lambda o\iota\ \tau\omega\nu\ \epsilon\kappa\kappa\lambda\eta\sigma\iota\omega\nu$) much of the foundation for Irvingite pretentions would have been destroyed. For the terms Bishops, Priest, (22) Deacons, Church, (23) Baptism, &c. I would wish to see substi-

"above a thought about it. Had they confined themselves to the "New Testament, what would they have found? Poor bishops "or overseers, recommended to work for their bread and to give "to the poor; one and the same with elders, only one name "showing the nature of the office, the other the kind of men to fill "it; and simple deacons to manage the charity of the Church." If these passages do not prove my recognition of these offices I know not what can.

(22) If by the word Priest be honestly meant nothing more than an abbreviation of Presbyter, though I cannot but suspect from the use made of this assumed name, much more is really meant than elder by most of those who adopt it, I have no other objection to it than its actually conveying a false idea to the minds of many.

(23) On what authority our author, in page 82, says "this is a Greek word signifying *the house of God*" I know not.

tuted the terms Overseers, Elders, Servants, Assembly, Immersion, &c.: and then the majority would have learnt to estimate the value of most of these words, much more justly than they now do. They would not have mistaken a youth for an elder, nor a christian teacher for one standing in the place of a jewish priest; Bishops would have appeared overseeing elders, and the title for office, would be found, not in their ordination or consecration by man, but in their possessing the qualifications mentioned by Paul to Timothy and Titus; and a church would be seen to be not an establishment united by creeds and canons, nor a building of brick and mortar, but an assembly of Christians or otherwise as those who compose it are met together in Christ's name or not. The assembly of Demetrius the Silversmith and his riotous heathens was a heathen εκκλησια or church, the assemblies of saints at Rome or Corinth, were christian εκκλησιαι or churches.

MAGISTRACY AND THE MILITARY PROFESSION.

As I cannot now go through all the subjects touched on by the author, I would say, that as to my view about magistracy and the military profession, I feel only disposed to say, he that can receive it, let him receive it; the subjects are not so brought forward in scripture, that I feel called upon to do more than I have done, my mind is unchanged for myself; but let every one be fully persuaded in his own mind, and I will not be his judge. But still I consider it necessary just to add the following remarks, relative to those passages of scripture, which our author considers conclusive. As to the case of John the Baptist, which is the only real case in point, it had nothing to do with the Gentile dispensation, but was like all the addresses of our

Lord, to the *lost sheep of the house of Israel*, to whom war was not only lawful, but often a duty as part of that law, which in its place, our Lord would have honored as much as commanding an offering to be made for cleansing or in being circumcised. I never held that war is essentially sinful, quite the reverse, as I have stated it was the duty of Jews, and will be that of Christians, in the day of their triumph, our exclusion from its exercise is during this dispensation. In the case of Cornelius, the only case that really bears as to *time*, being after the Gentile legislation from heaven had begun, we see not as in John the Baptist's command to the soldiers, any direction how the profession was to be carried on, but simple silence. Now it is quite natural to suppose that in communicating the first germs of truth to so young a convert, that that subject for the present should be passed by; what christian now, when first consulted by a soldier, just awakened to the importance of Jesus, as the hope of all the ends of the earth, would commence with the unlawfulness of his profession? and not endeavour rather so to lead him into all that is treasured up in Jesus, that these things would all fall from him as leaves in autumn. But what the ancient church felt on this point may be gathered from the following quotations. Gibbon says, " The christians were not less averse to the business " than to the pleasures of this world. The defence " of our persons and property they knew not how to " reconcile with the patient doctrine which enjoined " an unlimited forgiveness of past injuries, and com- " manded them to invite the repetition of fresh in- " sults. Their simplicity was offended by the use of

" oaths, by the pomp of magistracy, and by the active
" contentions of public life, nor could their humane
" ignorance be convinced, that it was lawful on any
" occasion to shed the blood of our fellow creatures,
" either by *the sword of justice*, or *by that of war;*
" even though their criminal or hostile attempts should
" threaten the peace and safety of the whole com-
" munity. It was acknowledged, that under a *less
" perfect law*, the Jewish constitution had been ex-
" ercised, with the approbation of Heaven, by inspired
" prophets and by anointed kings. The christians
" felt and confessed, that such institutions might be
" necessary for the present system of the world, and
" they *cheerfully submitted to the authority of their
" pagan governors*. But while they *inculcated the
" maxims of passive obedience, they refused to take
" any active part in the civil administration or the
" military defence of the empire*. Some indulgence
" might perhaps be allowed to those persons who,
" before their conversion, were already engaged
" in such violent and sanguinary occupations; but
" it was impossible that the christians, without re-
" nouncing a more sacred duty, could assume the char-
" acter of *soldiers*, of *magistrates*, or of *princes*. This
" indolent, or even criminal disregard to the public
" welfare, exposed them to the contempt and re-
" proaches of the Pagans, who very frequently asked,
" what must be the fate of the empire, attacked on
" every side by the barbarians, if all mankind should
" adopt the pusillanimous sentiments of the new sect ?
" To this insulting question the christian apologists
" returned obscure and ambiguous answers, as they

"were unwilling to reveal the secret cause of their
"security, the *expectation that, before the conver-
"sion of mankind was accomplished, war, govern-
"ment, the Roman empire, and the world itself,
"would be no more.*" (24) Again the bishop of Bristol in his ecclesiastial history of the second and third centuries says—" It is evident, from various pas-
"sages of Tertullian's works, that he deemed the ex-
"ercise of the functions of the *magistracy* incompati-
"ble with the profession of christianity; not merely
"on account of the danger to which, under a Pagan
"government, a magistrate was continually exposed,
"of being betrayed into some idolatrous act; but also
"because the dress and other insignia savoured of
"*those pomps and vanities, those works of the devil,*
"*which christians renounce at their baptism.* He
"does not expressly say that capital punishments
"are prohibited by the Gospel; but he certainly
"thought that christians ought not to *sit as judges in*
"*criminal causes*, or attend the amphitheatre, or be
"present at an execution. In the Treatise de Coro-
"nâ he enters into a regular discussion of the question,
"whether it is allowable for a christian to engage in
"the *military profession*. This question he *deter-
"mines in the negative.*" (25) The above testimony is ample so far as to shew what the views of the primitive Church were upon the subject, and I do truly believe as a general truth, that " he that taketh the
" sword shall perish by the sword," and that " the
" faith and patience of the saints" is manifested more

(24) Gibbon's Roman empire, p. 286.
(25) Eccles. Hist. pp. 363, 364.

by refusing the sword than by using it, and that if the saints would really overcome it, must be " by the " blood of the Lamb, by the word of their testimony " and not loving their lives unto the death."

ON FORSAKING ALL FOR CHRIST.

On giving up all, the author thinks it may be right for me to do it for myself, but that I ought not to urge it upon others. I have endeavoured not to do more than express Christ's words; our author says, that the command to the young man was a particular precept given to the young man because of his covetousness, this to me is mere supposition, because, Christ himself makes it general by his application " how " hardly shall *they that have riches* enter into the king- " dom of heaven." And our author then says, there is no other general precept in scripture to the same effect; but that in Luke xii. when Christ says to his disciples: " fear not little flock, it is your Father's good pleasure " to give you the kingdom, sell that ye have and " give alms, provide yourselves bags that wax not old, " a treasure in the Heavens that faileth not where no " thief approacheth, neither moth corrupteth, for where " your treasure is there your heart will be also." But if even these were all, are they not enough? has he half as much in the whole New Testament for the sabbath, for human ordination, for infant baptism, and does not the author press these points? But further it is written " let this mind be in you which was also in " Christ Jesus, who being in the form of God, thought " it not robbery to be equal with God, yet *made him-* " *self* of no reputation (or emptied himself). For

" ye know the grace of our Lord Jesus Christ, that
" though he was rich, yet for your sakes he became
" poor, that ye through his poverty might be rich."
And when I hear our Lord's commendation of the poor
widow for giving *all that she had even all her living*
not to a *present urgent case of need*, but for casting it
into the public treasury of God, because it was of *her
penury:* and when I see Barnabas and all the Church at
Jerusalem acting literally on these precepts immediately after the out-pouring of the Holy Ghost upon
them, I feel it happier and safer to take them for guides,
than to reason away the plainest exhortations of scripture supported by the example of the Head of the
Church, and those so closely connected with Him, when
I feel in my heart so many natural reasons to take the
other side of the question, and seeing also, that it is
the same the Gentiles do, who know not our God and
Father. Yet against any one's will, I have no wish to
press so great a privilege, as being poor with Christ
and for Christ, for he is too rich to need and too sensible to motives to receive with pleasure that which is
not given from love. Here our author has suggested
all possible base motives, as probably actuating those
who give up, how easy would it be to retort the insinuation, and shew the probable causes of the blindness
of those who retain. If any one would wish to see the
operation of this retaining system, and the effect, the
contemplation of it had on one whose sphere of observation was second to none ; let him read the following
remarks from that good man John Wesley, as if despairing, not only of methodism, but christianity itself;
he says " How astonishing a thing is this ? How can

" we understand it? Does it not seem (and yet this
" cannot be) that christianity, true scriptural christi-
" anity, has a tendency in process of time to undeter-
" mine and destroy itself? For wherever true chris-
" tianity spreads, it must cause diligence and frugality,
" which in the natural course of things must beget
" riches; and riches naturally beget pride, love of the
" world and every temper that is destructive of chris-
" tianity. Now if there be no way to prevent this,
" christianity is inconsistent with itself, and of conse-
" quence cannot stand, cannot continue long among
" any people, since wherever it generally prevails, it
" saps its own foundation." He saw not the antidote
that the command to *give* is *co-extensive with the command to get*, here is the cure of this root of all evil to labour with your own hands, *to have to give to him that needeth*. (26)

HEBREW CRITICISMS.

I now desire to quit all these disconnected remarks and apply simply to the subject of the Law. The order I propose to pursue is, first, to examine our author's He-

(26.) On the command not to lay up and others equally unpalatable to the natural mind of man our Author thinks Bishop Pearse has just hit the point when he turns lay not up treasures on earth into a form of Hebrew speech, notwithstanding all the New Testament precepts and abundant examples in support of its literal acceptation. He also thinks to turn the other cheek would only be to irritate, yet I knew a child of God who whilst pressing on a Jew the reception of Jesus, so irritated him that the Jew knocked him down and when he arose he said with great meekness " Strike me but only hear me" and this so overpowered the Jew that it became the means of his conversion. It is the spirit in which the thing is done and not the doing of it that irritates.

brew criticism, from the old Testament, then his Greek from the new, where, if I apprehend the meaning of words, we shall find not only " mere assertion" as the author accuses me of, but *false* assertion to an extent that astonishes me, after having set these two points at rest, I propose dwelling a little at large on some other points that I think it important to endeavour to put in a clear point of view. The distinction our Author endeavours to draw from Hebrew phrasealogy to support the divisions of the law into what he calls " our technical arrangement into moral, ceremonial, and judicial" appears to me an ideal distinction and wholly unsupported by scripture, and to any one who desires proof of this, I would advise going through the Hebrew words in Taylor's Hebrew concordance or our Author's translations of them in italics (in pages 21 and 22) in Cruden; and I feel assured, that no unbiased mind will hesitate a moment in coming to the conclusion, that the Holy Spirit uses all the words referred to for all, and any part of the law; or at least that there is no word that can be shewn to be exclusively applied to any one part of the law; whether the Decalogue, or " the moral, ceremonial or judicial" parts of it. But I shall notwithstanding adduce one or two examples of each word to shew how untenable the distinctions are.

1st. The author says:

" עדוּת (ædooth) testimony in the singular, (27) is solely applied to the Decalogue," again " This word then appears to be without a single exception the proper and distinctive name of the decalogue. p. 21."

(27.) Gesenius in his Hebrew Lexicon renders this word "1. ordinance, institution" and " 2. Law i. q. תּוֹרָה."

Now in Ps. lxxxi. 3—5. it is said. "Blow up the "trumpet in the new moons, in the time appointed, on "our solemn feast day." (comp. Num. 10. 10. Lev. 23. 24. &c. &c.) "For *this* was a statute חק khok for "Israel and a law מִשְׁפָּט mishpat of the God of Jacob. "*This* he ordained in Joseph for a *Testimony* עֵדוּת "ædooth (in the singular) when he went out of the "land of Egypt." Is blowing of trumpets a part of the Decalogue? compare also 2 Kings 11. 12 and 2 Chron. 23. 11. with Deut. 17, 18, 19, 20, &c.

2ndly Again he says,

"בְּרִית bereeth covenant, also is never applied to the ceremonial law. When it signifies, law, and not a contract it is restricted to law of the ten commandments." p. 22.

In 2, Kings 2. 21. it is said "the King commanded all the people saying "keep the passover unto the Lord your God: as it is written in the book of this covenant" בְּרִית bereeth, from which it is evident that "the book of this covenant" must have contained at least parts of the sacrificial law, else how could the proper mode of observing the passover have been learnt from it, but further by a comparison of verse 8 of the preceding chapter with the 2d verse of this we see that "the book of the covenant" סֵפֶר הַבְּרִית sepher habbereeth is the same as "the book of the law" סֵפֶר הַתּוֹרָה sepher hattorah which we shall presently prove to comprehend the whole law of Moses, or at least, not solely the Decalogue. I would here say something on the expressions "Ark of the Testimony" or "Ark of the Covenant" which is so called Iagree

with our Author, in thinking " because it contained the 10 Commandments," (p. 21) for it must not be forgotten, that my whole argument has not been against applying either עֵדוּת ædooth testimony or בְּרִית bereeth covenant to the decalogue in their proper place, but against the assertion that they are exclusively so applied; upon which restriction alone, this part of our author's argument rests. But I will now go further and prove, that even though this restricted sense could be established, it never was intended as an indication, that the ark of the covenant or covenant contained in the ark was to be perpetual, for in Jeremiah it is said after promising the Jews their final restoration and blessing. " It shall come to pass, when ye be multi-
" plied and increased in the land, *in those days*, saith
" the Lord, *they shall say no more, the ark of the*
" *covenant* (אֲרוֹן בְּרִית aron bereeth) *of the Lord:*
" *neither shall it come to mind: neither shall they*
" *remember it; neither shall they visit it;* neither shall
" that be done any more. At that time they shall call
" Jerusalem the throne of the Lord; and all the nations
" shall be gathered unto it, to the name of the Lord,
" to Jerusalem: neither shall they walk any more after
" the imagination of their evil heart. In those days
" the house of Judah shall walk with the house of
" Israel, and they shall come together out of the land
" of the north to the land that I have given for an
" inheritance unto your fathers." (ch. iii. 16,18.) Now surely, no language can be clearer than this, nor prove more to a demonstratiom, that the Gentiles never could be put under, as a rule of life, or justification, a law which

even by the Jews was to be forgotten when they are brought back, as they will be under the new covenant, as Jeremiah says " Behold, the days come, saith the
" Lord, that I will make a new covenant with the
" house of Israel, and with the house of Judah: not
" according to the covenant that I made with their
" fathers in the day that I took them by the hand to
" bring them out of the land of Egypt; which my
" covenant they break, although I was an husband un-
" to them, saith the Lord; but this shall be the cove-
" nant that I will make with the house of Israel;
" After those days, saith the Lord, I will put my law
" in their inward parts, and write it in their hearts;
" and will be their God, and they shall be my people."
(ch. xxxi. 31 33.) But this is the very convenant in which believers in this dispensation are placed by Paul, who, when quoting these very words of Jeremiah, says,
" But now hath he obtained a more excellent ministry,
" by how much also he is the mediator of a better cove-
" nant, which was established upon better promises.
" For if that first covenant had been faultless, there
" should no place have been sought for the second.
" For finding fault with them, he saith, Behold, the
" days come, saith the Lord, when I will make a new
" covenant with the house of Israel and with the house
" of Judah: not according to the covenant that I made
" with their fathers in the day when I took them by
" the hand to lead them out of the land of Egypt; be-
" cause they continued not in my covenant, and I re-
" garded them not, saith the Lord. For this is the
" covenant that I will make with the house of Israel
" after those days, saith the Lord; I will put my laws

"into their mind, and write them in their hearts: and
"I will be to them a God, and they shall be to me a
"people: and they shall not teach every man his
"neighbour, and every man his brother, saying, know
"the Lord: for all shall know me, from the least to the
"greatest. For I will be merciful to their unrighte-
"ousness, and their sins and their iniquities will I re-
"member no more. In that he saith, A new covenant;
"he hath made the first old. Now that which decay-
"eth and waxeth old, is ready to vanish away." (Heb.
"viii. 6—13.) And again he says " by one offering he
"hath perfected for ever them that are sanctified.
"Whereof the Holy Ghost also is a witness to us: for
"after that he had said before, this is the covenant
"that I will make with them after those days, saith
"the Lord, I will put my laws into their hearts, and in
"their minds will I write them; and their sins and ini-
"quities will I remember no more. Now where remis-
"sion of these is, there is no more offering for sin."
(Heb. x. 14—18.) Here then we see Jeremiah pro-
phetically sets forth that on the introduction of the new
covenant, the old covenant kept in the Ark, shall neither
come into mind, nor be remembered, because, as Paul
says in the 2. Cor. iii. that the covenant written and en-
graved on stones, which was to be done away had no
glory, by reason of the glory that excelleth and remaineth; now, because the transcendant glory of the
new covenant has not by its surpassing excellencies
superseded the old one, contained in the Ark, so as
to cause it to be forgotten and clean gone out of the
mind of those, who hold the views of our author as Jeremiah said it should do, on the introduction of the

new covenant; we may see plainly, that they have come short in their view of the glory of the name of that Lord, whose name was to be in Jerusalem, the sole object round which all the nations were to gather, for the isles were to wait for *His* law, and not to have their eyes again directed to the Ark, or the old covenant it contained; but to Jesus the mediator of the new covenant, and as the Father said, Him they were to hear. For I think all will allow that if this covenant contained in the Ark is to be our rule of life, it never can become as Jeremiah says it shall when the Lord shall be manifested in Jerusalem, a thing that should neither be remembered nor come into mind. (28) But this is not all; not only does this view harmonize with what Paul says in Rom. vii, Gal. iv, and 2 Cor. iii: but when the prophet Ezekial is describing most minutely the temple into which the Prince is to return from the east, there is no Ark of the covenant even mentioned, so consistent' is truth with itself. When he came as the light of the Gentiles, and for whose law they were to wait, who was the brightness of his Father's glory and the express image of his person, and Jerusalem became the throne of the Lord, even that Jerusalem which is above the mother of us all, we had nothing more to do with the ark of the covenant neither should it be remembered by us, or be upon our hearts, or come into mind by reason of that everlasting covenant es-

(28) Bishop Lowth in this place evidently had the same view of the passage, and the cause of its being forgotten, and refers his readers to Gal. iv: but the latter part of Heb. xiii. is yet more striking, as shewing the connection in the mind of the spirit, between the heavenly Jerusalem legislation from thence and the obedience supremely required to it.

tablished upon better promises in the hand of a better mediator. But to proceed,

3d. In page 42, the author says:

"The place in Rom. vii. 12. 'wherefore the law is holy, and the commandment holy, and just, and good,' shews the perpetuity of the law. Here νομος law, answers to תורה torah and indicates the moral law in general, the two tables: and εντολη as above mentioned, answers to חק khok commandment, to indicate the separate precepts. Not only the law generally, but every separate command is holy. He does not say that it was holy under the Jewish dispensation, and that it has ceased to be so now; he positively says, it is now holy. That it is the moral law, which St. Paul means, is proved by his quotation of it, 'Thou shalt not covet.'

From the above it would seem that תורה torah referred solely to the Moral Law whereas its primary signification is an *instruction* or *precept* of any kind (as of a parent) (see Prov. 1. 8. 3. 1. &c.) secondarily (29) *a law* in which sense it is also used of sacrifices, thus in Lev. vii. 7. the Lord says to Moses " as " the sin offering is, so is the trespass offering: " there is one law תורה torah for them." See also Lev. vi. 9, 14, 25. &c. In Neh. xiii. 1—3: it is used of the law respecting the Moabites and Ammonites mentioned in Deut. xxiii. 3, 4. The expression " the book of the law" ספר התורה sepher hattorah occurs in many places, where it unquestionably refers to the whole law of Moses: among other texts see the following, Deut. xxxi. 24. 26; Jos. viii. 34; 2. Kin.

(29) See Gesnius subvoce.

xxii. 8, 11; as in fact it is used by the Jews in the present day who know nothing of the present scholastic divisions of their law. (30) The Jews also very commonly call the whole, old Testament, by this word תורה torah; so much for the three words which our Author says, apply exclusively to the decalogue.

4th. The Author now comes to those words which he would make apply exclusively to the other parts of the law, and says:

"On the contrary, the words that are employed by the sacred writers to denote those parts of the law, which we denominate ceremonial and judicial, are חקים kharkkeem *statutes*, פקודים pekoodeem *precepts*, מצום mitzvoth commands, עדות ædooth in the plural *testimonies*, and משפטים mishpateem *judgments*."

I would here refer to the 5th of Deut. the 1st and the following verses. It is said (verse 1.) "and Moses called all Israel and said unto them, Hear, O Israel the *statutes*, חקים khukkeem, and the *judgments* משפטים mishpateem, which I speak in your ears this day;" that which is called here the statutes and judgments, we find from the following verses (vi. 21.) to include the decalogue. Again in Deut. vi.

(30) It is plain from the Masonetic notes at the end of the Pentateuch that the Masorites applied this word תורה torah to the whole of that book; and Van der Hooght in the preface to his Hebrew bible, says " Titulo תורה torah *Legis* comprehenduntur "quinque LIBRI Mosis ut בראשית Genesis, שמות Exodus. " ויקרא Leviticus במדבר Numeri, et דברים Deuteronomium."

1, 2, 17. besides judgments and statutes mentioned before, the words *commandments* מִצְוֹת mitzooth and *testimonies* עֵדוֹת ædooth are also used with the same meaning, referring to those moral precepts contained in the sixth chapter which has nothing to do with anything, either ceremonial or judicial. With regard to the word פִּקּוּדִים pekkoodeem *precepts* it is not as far as I can find used once in the old Testament, except in the Psalms, where it occurs about thirty times, as in Ps. cix. 4, 15, 27, 45, &c;—yet, so far from being exclusively applied to any one part of the law, more than to another, it seems to refer to the whole will of God whensoever and howsoever revealed to man, and to correspond to the words *law* (תּוֹרָה torah) *testimonies, statutes*, &c. used in the same Psalm. To any person who felt interested in the enquiry I would recommend the reading of the 119th Psalm (where almost all the words in question are used) in order to be assured that whatever distinctions man may make for the sake of argument, the scripture has made none. According to our author, most of that beautiful Psalm which believers generally consider to refer to the obedience God, requires of them to his *whole* manifested will, would simply relate to that which belongs to what he " terms those parts of the law which we denominate ceremonial and judicial."

In concluding these remarks on the above Hebrew words, I would add, that our author in page 42, where he would prove " the perpetuity of the law," from Rom. 7. 12, compares the Greek word εντολη with the Hebrew word חק khok, the singular of חקים khukkeem; which, according to p. 22, he refers to the ceremonial or judicial parts of the law; and consequently this verse must prove not only the perpetuity of the moral law; (which he says, תורה torah indicates) but also the perpetuity of those parts of the law he terms ceremonial and judicial. If we suppose the assertion, that the Hebrew word חק khok, answers to the Greek word εντολη in this place as an oversight, it proves at least that the author himself could have had no very accurate perception of the distinction between the words the difference of which he had just before been trying to establish, else he would have felt that חק khok, did not convey the idea he evidently designed it should.

The Author after having made the above unwarrantable and untrue assertions respecting the distinctions which he desired to draw from scripture phraseology, in support of his theory of the division of the Mosaic law, into moral, ceremonial, and judicial, has the following remarks:—

" This is a very remarkable distinction; and deserves
" the most serious notice, as clearly indicating the inten-
" tion of the Holy Spirit relative to that law which is holy,
" just and good, in contradistinction to that which was to
" pass away.......Now, is not this evidently design?
" Why should there be such uniformity in the application
" of these two words? Surely for no other purpose, but to
" set apart and distinguish the moral law, from the law of
" rites and ceremonies. From this it may appear, how false
" is Mr. Groves's assertion;—' Nor is there any thing in
" the phraseology of scripture to lead to the distinctions

" made so much of.' The very phraseology of scripture
" sanctions this distinction."

The above criticisms abundantly prove the untenable nature of our Author's assertions upon this head, but had the distinction attempted to be set up by our author been proved to be as true as it is indisputably false, still he would have been as far as ever from having proved that the Decalogue was designed to stand apart from the other two, so that, when they were abrogated or disannulled, this alone was to remain in force. For in the New Testament, passages are adopted from all parts alike; " thou shalt not muzzle the ox that treadeth out the corn," is as much embodied to teach us to support those who minister the word of life, as " Honour thy father and mother" is to teach us to do them service, though the one is taken from the Decalogue, the other not; and the history of the rebellion of the children of Israel in the wilderness recounted in 1 Cor. x. is plainly *declared to be written* to teach us not to be idolaters, fornicators, tempters of God or murmerers, and therefore to be as " all scripture is," a profitable guide, and consequently if quoting " thou shalt not covet" proves the decalogue as a whole to be in force; on the same principle, the quoting of these parts of the judicial or civil law, proves they are all still in force.

GREEK CRITICISMS.

I shall now proceed to consider our author's New Testament criticisms, and ill supplied as I find myself with books for a literary research yet I think I shall be able to shew that the carelessness which I have shewn to exist in the Hebrew criticism of our author hardly exceeds that manifested in the Greek.

Let us now consider the remarks of our author on the Vth of Matthew, which he seems to think I have treated with great brevity, and he seems to infer, because it had given him great difficulty to reconcile parts of it with his system, that therefore it would be difficult with mine; whereas I see no difficulty in the chapter at all. It is evident that in consequence of our Lord's disregard for traditional Judaism, the Pharisees of his time went about from the beginning to the end of his life to accuse him as a breaker of the Law, and a profaner of the Sabbath, because he confined himself to what was written and would not give place to their bigotted and learned ignorance for one moment, in things that regarded his Father's word, and our Lord foreseeing this from the beginning of his ministry, and to prevent his disciples being in any way deceived as to his real design or to be led themselves into breaches of the law, under the notion, that he disregarded any thing that was really his Father's in it, says " think not I am come to destroy the " Law or the Prophets. I am not come to destroy, " but to fulfil." Here then is a plain statement of the object of Christ's coming, namely, to fulfil the Law and the Prophets, which he either has done, or not accomplished the end of his Mission; but this, after great labour and thought, the author seems himself to have arrived at, Christ then goes on to say " *For* verily I say " unto you, till heaven and earth pass, *one jot* " *or one tittle* shall in no wise pass from *the Law* till " all be fulfilled" or till all things come to pass. Now the word " for" in the commencement of this last sentence shews a strong reason, why, what was stated in the preceding sentence could, not but take place, the Law and prophets must have a complete fulfilment, in that which concerns Him previous to the passing away of *one jot or one tittle of the law;* and the clause, till heaven and earth pass away is just synonymous with the corresponding passage in Luke, where, instead of the above form of words we have simply "it is easier for heaven and earth to pass away, than one tittle of the Law to fail." Again our Lord says on another occasion, heaven and earth shall pass away, but my word shall not pass away. But our Lord does not only declare the impossibility of the Law passing away before its accomplishment, but he declares the indivisibility of the Law, *not one jot or one tittle* was to pass away till all was fulfilled: either then it is all gone or none, for that is the condition of the declaration the integrity and indivisibility of *the Law*. Our author here found it necessary to limit the meaning of the word, law, used by our Lord to the ten commandments and the pains he bestows on the attempt, and the assertions with which he endeavours to support it, make it necessary to dwell here for a few moments. Our author's assertions here are two; first, that though ὀνομος law *sometimes* may mean more than the decalogue, yet, that here it ought not, because, secondly; our Lord in the chapter immediately afterwards quotes *only* from the decalogue. Now both these are worthy of the criticism of this pamphlet. After having discovered the extreme inaccuracy of our author's assertions, relative to the use of the Hebrew, he introduces into his pamphlet, I was led on the word ὁ νομος to open, Trommeus and found that so far from ο νομος or law, having the restricted meaning of the decalogue as a general meaning, in about 50 places where the word occurs in the Pentateuch in 45, it has to do indisputably with the ceremonial law only, and in the other 4 or 5 it is difficult to say it had any restricted meaning to the decalogue. And the second assertion of our author is equally unfounded, that the decalogue only is quoted by our Lord in the chapter that follows. There are seven quotations which I shall presently introduce, and of which *seven*, only TWO are from the decalogue. But this criticism of our author is not only overthrown by the palpable inaccuracy of the assertions on which it rested, but by the direct statement of our Lord himself who has shown what he meant by the law being fulfilled in his reference to this conversation in Luke xxiv. 25, 27, 44 and 47, where he exclaims "O fools, and slow " of heart to believe *all* that the prophets have spoken : " ought not Christ to have suffered these things, and to " enter into his glory? and beginning at Moses and " all the prophets, he expounded unto them in all the " scriptures the things concerning himself." And after having pointed to his pierced hands and feet as the seals of the fulfilment, he said " *these are the* " *words which I spake unto you, while I was yet with* " *you,* that *all things* τα παντα must be fulfilled, which " were written in the law of Moses, and in the Pro" phets, and in the Psalms, concerning me. Then " opened he their understanding, that they might un" derstand the scriptures, and said unto them, thus " it is written, and thus it behoved Christ to suffer, " and to rise from the dead the third day : and that " repentance and remission of sins should be preach-

"ed in his name, among all nations, beginning at Je-
"rusalem, and ye are witnesses of these things. And,
"behold, I send the promise of my Father upon you;
"but tarry ye in the city of Jerusalem, until ye be
"endued with power from on high." Now in these
remarkable verses, we see first, what our Lord meant,
when he said, he came not to abrogate but *fulfil*.
Here you see that the *all things* τα παντα upon which
our author endeavours to put the meaning, the final
consummation of all things is quoted again by our
Lord from his conversation in Matthew as having reference *to all things* written in the law of Moses, and
in the Prophets, and in the Psalms concerning him, so
that the *all things come into being* (ἕως ἂν παντα
γενηται) or are finished in Matthew the 5th, 18, our
Lord makes evidently the same as the all things
must be fulfilled "οτι δει πληρωθηναι παντα τα γεγραμ
μενα" in Luke xxiv. 44 : but here our Lord shews that
the τα παντα had no reference to the final consummation of all things as our author so unhesitatingly without a shadow of evidence assumes; but the all things
written concerning him. But this passage not only
shews what the all things were that he had fulfilled
but it shews us that as Moses went up into the mount
and received the law from the hands of the Lord 50
days after the offering up of the typical paschal Lamb.
So Christ's disciples were to wait in Jerusalem till
their Lord had ascended into the presence of his
Father. And at the end of 50 days from the offering
up of Himself as the true paschal Lamb, He promulgated his new Testament established upon
better promises; to be preached in all the

world, beginning at Jerusalem. And as the other testament was written on stones, by God's finger, this was to be written on his disciples hearts by God's Spirit. For in fact the work of atonement was not finished till by his own blood; he entered into the Holy place before his Father, just as the High Priest on the day of atonement, finished not the services of that memorable day, till he carried the blood of the sacrifice in before the mercy seat in the Holy place, the typical heaven within the veil, and that *Heaven* is the place from whence Christ is regarded as promulgating his new law, not expounding the old one of Sinai, the following passage in the Hebrews, proves wherein the Spirit says, " See that " ye refuse not him that speaketh. For if they escaped " not who refused him that spoke on earth, much more " shall not we escape if we turn away from him *that* " *speaketh from heaven.*" ch. xii. 25.

Our author has asserted, that our Lord only quotes the Decalogue, after these remarks on the law. The fact is, our Lord goes on to teach his disciples, what their *present* duty was as perfect Jews who were his disciples, not only, not to break the law in one of its least commandments, or to teach men so, but so to fulfil them that their righteousness in them should surpass that of the Scribes and Pharisees, if they would enter into the kingdom of Heaven, that is his kingdom. Our Lord then goes on to explain what he means by his disciples exceeding in righteousness the Scribes and Pharisees. He goes on to say (1) ye have heard that it was said *to* them (not by) of old time thou shalt not kill, and, whoever shall kill, shall be in danger of the Judgment, but I say *unto* you, whosoever is angry with his brother

&c. (2) ye have heard that it was said to them of old time, thou shalt not commit adultery; but I say *unto you*, that whosoever looketh on a woman to lust after her, hath committed adultery already with her in his heart. (3) It has been said whoever shall put away his wife, let him give her a writing of divorcement; but I say unto you, that whosoever shall put away his wife except for the cause of fornication, committeth adultery, &c. (4) Again ye have heard that it hath been said *to* them of old time, thou shalt not forswear thyself, but shalt perform unto the Lord thine oath; but I say *unto you*, swear not at all, &c. (5) Ye have heard that it hath been said, an eye for an eye, and a tooth for a tooth; but I say unto you, that ye resist not evil. (6) Ye have heard that it hath been said, thou shalt love thy neighbour and (7) hate thine enemies, &c.

Here then our Lord has shown what he meant by telling his disciples their righteousness must exceed that of the Scribes and Pharisees. How the author of the Perpetuity of the Law in p. 34, can make the following assertion I leave him to explain. "Our Saviour *in all this* chapter immediately after the utterance of these words recites ONLY the Precepts of the *moral* law;" by which he says, "he means the Decalogue and though he acknowledges he quotes an eye for an eye and a tooth for a tooth, yet he only allows this to have been an explanatory one on the 6th commandment: now, who would believe that Our Lord quotes seven separate texts, of which only, two are from the Decalogue. Before I dismiss the subject I must make a few remarks on our Lord's quotation "and hate thine enemy." With my saying this is a general precept when the author thinks it is particular, he appears to express himself with great apparent indignation, to this I have only to say, that all our Lord's preceding quotations are quoted verbatim from Moses' words, and therefore if I attribute to our Lord a right understanding of this passage, and if he applies it generally, I think there is no great crime in my thinking he knew the extent of the original enactment better than I, and if the word hate is allowed, a mitigated sense in such passages as he that hateth not father and mother, and he that hateth not his own life, Jacob have I loved and Esau have I hated; I see not why, according to the analogy of the Scriptures all indited by the same Lord, it may not be allowed here. The author thinks I must mean Deut. xxiii. 6, where it is said that a Moabite and an Ammonite were to be hated because they opposed God's people, but I also mean, Ezra ix. 1, where the Cannanites, Hittites, Perizzites, Jebusites, Ammonites, Moabites, Egyptians are also included in the list, as it is shown in the 12 verse " Give not your daughters to their sons, nor take their sons to your daughters, neither *seek their peace nor their wealth for ever.*" Here then I think I see a full explanation on general principles of that which was applied originally towards Moab and Ammon only. And it is my full conviction that our Lord in quoting the term generally as he did, was only quoting the mind of the Spirit in that passage in Deuteronomy, and David in the 139 Psalm enters into the full expression of this sentiment, when he says, " Do " not I hate them, O Lord, that hate thee? and am " not I grieved with those that rise up against thee? " I hate them with perfect hatred: I count them

"mine enemies." (ver. 21, 22) Here I think as well as in a multitude of other places in the Psalms, the Spirit teaches fully the hatred of *national* enemies among the Jews, and evidently because they were regarded in their attacks on God's land and God's people as rebelling against Him, to whom both belonged in an especial manner. If this does not satisfy the author, I have no desire to say more than that I shall rather take the Lord's meaning of the passage in Deuteronomy, than any other interpretation. Now all these literal quotations of the words used by Moses *to* the ancients, and as such evidently quoted by our Lord, our author asserts to be merely glosses; surely, when our Lord wanted to attack the glosses of the Pharisees, he quotes the text against their gloss, for instance in Mark vii. 61—3. " He answered and said
" unto them, well hath Esaias prophesied of you hy-
" pocrites, as it is written, This people honoreth me
" with their lips, but their heart is far from me. How-
" beit in vain do they worship me, teaching for doc-
" trines the commandments of men. For laying aside
" the commandment of God, ye hold the tradition of
" men, as the washing of pots and cups: and many
" other such like things ye do, and he said unto them,
" Full well he reject the commandment of God, that
" ye may keep your own tradition. For Moses said,
" Honour thy father and thy mother, and whoso curs-
" eth father or mother, let him die the death. But
" ye say, If a man shall say to his father or mother it
" is corban, that is to say a gift, by whatsoever thou
" mightest be profited by me, he shall be free. And
" ye suffer him no more to do ought for his father or

" his mother; making the word of God of none effect
" through your tradition, which ye have delivered:
" and many such like things do ye." Again, Mat. xxiii.
16—22. " Woe unto you, ye blind guides, which
" say, whosoever shall swear by the temple, it is no-
" thing; but whosoever shall swear by the gold of the
" temple, he is a debtor! Ye fools and blind: for
" whether is greater, the gold, or the temple, that
" sanctifieth the gold? And whosoever shall swear
" by the altar, it is nothing; but whosoever sweareth
" by the gift that is upon it, he is guilty. Ye fools
" and blind: for whether is greater the gift, or the al-
" tar that sanctifieth the gift? Whoso therefore shall
" swear by the altar, sweareth by it, and by all things
" thereon. And whoso shall swear by the temple,
" sweareth by it, and by him that dwelleth therein.
" And he that shall swear by heaven, sweareth by the
" throne of God, and by him that sitteth thereon."
Here the glosses of the Pharisees are dealt with truly,
but how different the language from that in the 5th
of Matthew. (31) But surely if our author can
turn six quotations of our Lord without a shadow of evidence into glosses of the Pharisees,
he may pardon me taking the 7th literally from the
lips of Jesus. I have not yet done with our author's
criticisms he makes the phrase " by them of old time"
synonymous with " by the Pharisees" to this translation however, my objection is two-fold: first, that it
should be translated " *by* them of old time" at all in-

(31) I may also here add that whenever the Evangelists or the
Jews refer to the authors of their traditions, they never use the
word αρχαιοι but πρεσβυτεροι as in Matt. xv. 2.

stead of " *to* them of old time" according to the universal usage of the fathers and all the translators, till Beza's time and even now I find the German translation, Campbell, Bishop Jebb, Rosenmuller are all against the " *by*" but I subjoin Campbell's note as conclusive. It is as follows: " That it was said *to the* " *ancients*, οτι ερρεθη τοις αρχαιοις English translation. That it was said by them of old time—Beza " Dictum " fuisse a veteribus. Beza was the FIRST interpreter " of the N. T. who made the ancients those *by* whom, " and not those *to* whom, the sentences here quoted " were spoken. These other Latin versions, the Vul Ar. " Er. Tu. Cas. Cal. and Pisc. are all against him. " Among the Protestant translators into modern tongues, " Beza whose work was much in vogue with the re- " formed, had his imitators Dio. in Itn. rendered it " che fu detto dagli antichi; the G. F. quil a ete dit " par les anciens, so also the common Eng. But *all* " *the English versions of an older date*, even that exe- " cuted at Geneva, say ' *to* them of old time.' Lu- " ther in like manner, in his German translation, says, " ' zu den alten,' I have a protestant translation in Itn. " and Fr. published by Giovan, Luigi, Paschale in " 1555, the year before the 1st edition of Beza's, " (the place not mentioned), which renders it in the " same way with " all preceding translators, without " exception, ' a gli antichi,' and ' aux anciens' all the " late translators French and English have returned " to the *uniform sense of* antiquity, rendering it *to*, " not *by* the ancients. For the meaning of a word or " phrase, which frequently occurs in scripture, the " first recourse ought to be to the sacred writers,

" especially the writer of the book where the passage
" occurs. Now the verb ρεω (and the same may be
" observed of its synonymes) in the passive voice,
" where the speaker or speakers are mentioned, has
" uniformly the speaker in the genitive case, preceded
" by the preposition ὑπο or δια. And in no book does
" this occur oftener than in Mat. see chap ii. 15,17,23.
" iii. 13. iv. 14. viii. 17. xii. 17. xiii. 35. xxi. 4. xxiv.
" 15. xxvii. 9. xxii. 31. In this last we have an exam-
" ple both of those to whom, and of him by whom,
" the thing was said, the former in the dative, the
" latter in the genitive with the preposition ὑπο. When
" the persons spoken to are mentioned, they are *invari-
" ably in the dative* Rom. ix. 12, 26. Gal. iii. 16.
" Apo. vi. 11. ix. 4. With such a number of examples
" on one side (yet these are not all,) and *not one from
" scripture on the opposite.* I should think it very as-
" suming in a translator, without the least necessity to
" reject the exposition given by all who had preceded
" him."

" Nor can anything account for such a palpable
" violence done the sacred text by a man of Beza's
" knowledge, but that he had too much of the polemic
" spirit, the epidemical disease of his time to be in
" all respects a faithful translator."

Again, I object to the application of the term
(τοις αρχαιοις) (those in the beginning) to the Pharisees who had not existed above a hundred years as
a sect. I feel also that merely to support this theory
to turn our Lord's verbal quotations of the old Testament into glosses of the Pharisees without a syllable
in the sacred text to support it, is treating the sacred

text with a force and violence which rather than do I would submit to any difficulties. I never before saw the power of prejudice in any case so strong and I trust I may now dismiss the point without being accused of slighting its difficulties. I feel it owes all its difficulties to the pre-conceived notions of those who come to it with the full conviction that it cannot mean what it says, and only busy themselves in making it at all hazards speak what *they think* it ought; now to allow the least weight to our author's reasoning you must concede to him the following points: 1st, that he may give to ὁ νομος (the law) a particularity of meaning it never bears; 2d, to give a shadow of weight to this you must allow him to assert as true against the clearest evidence that after this word in the whole chapter, our Lord quotes from nothing, but the decalogue; 3d, you must allow him to translate τοις αρχαιοις so as to mean *by the Pharisees* (contrary to the universal usage of the language as I have shewn) instead of *to the ancients;* 4th, you must allow τα παντα (all things) to mean the final consummation of all things contrary to our Lord's own interpretation of the meaning of his own words, Luke xxiv. 44. where he confines the meaning to the things he had fulfilled and which were written in Moses and the Prophets and the Psalms concerning him; 5th, And to sum up the whole you must allow him to turn our Lord's literal quotations from Moses without the shadow of evidence into glosses of the Pharisees.

I trust I have shewn sufficiently clearly the futility of those criticisms of our author, on which the division of the law was by him attempted to be founded. Let us now examine into the foundation our author has for what he retains and undertakes to defend in the following sentence, in page 27, he says:

"We do not undertake to defend anything but the ten commandments written with God's own finger, spoken by God's own mouth, preserved in God's own house, the tabernacle, and deposited beneath his own stated and fixed residence in that tabernacle, the ark, as if he wished to have it perpetually near himself, being the image of his own eternal divinity."

There is something verbally imposing in this sentence, but really the whole covenant was spoken by God's own mouth, preserved in God's own house, the tabernacle in the holiest of all deposited beneath his own stated and fixed residence in that tabernacle beside the ark, as if he wished to have it perpetually near himself with the manna in the golden pot and Aaron's rod that budded. The decalogue being put within the ark seemed to be a summary of the covenant between God and Israel as to the terms upon which they held the land so long as they nationally avoided those sins of the nations whose land they were going to inhabit; because of whose sins they were to possess the land, but if they became idolators or dishonored their parents, they were not to dwell on the land which the Lord gave them; when therefore they fell into idolatry and were dispersed, their ark was lost and their title deed of inheritance written with God's own hands, lost with it; and as Jeremiah declares and Ezekiel shews it has no place under the new covenant, nor shall ever come again into mind. That the decalogue did not contain the greatest moral truth of the Sinai covenant is evident from our blessed Lord's quotations when asked, what were the two great commandments in the law. He referred to no command in the decalogue deposited within the ark, but to Deut. vi. 5. and to Lev. xix. 18. Jesus said unto him; Thou shalt love the Lord thy God with all thy heart, and with all thy soul, and with all thy mind, this is the first and great commandment; and the second is like unto it; Thou shalt love thy neighbour as thyself: on these two commandments hang all the law and the prophets. Paul shews us also how love is the fulfilling of the law both in the 1 Cor. xiii. and also in Rom. x. in this he shews how when it works negatively it fulfils the law of the second table; but if you would see it working negatively and positively you must go to 1 Cor. xiii. If our author or any others will have that "Thou shalt not worship other gods, &c." comprehends "Thou shalt love the Lord thy God with all thy heart and soul and mind" and thou shalt not kill, steal, nor covet; " thou shalt love thy neighbour as thyself," arguments at all events would be useless. There is however in the passage above, a very clear statement of our author's position, the separation of the decalogue from the rest of the system of the Jewish legislation. I think I have already proved sufficiently clearly, that the word of God itself gives no ground for this division of one part from another. And I might say is it not strange if the Decalogue were left as a whole binding on the Gentiles and if it were to this the Gentiles were to look and not to their own Jesus speaking to them from heaven, is it not strange I say that it is never once referred to as such in all the apostolic writings nor for centuries afterwards, and that not for want of occasions on which it was necessary for when certain Jews went down from Jerusalem to Antioch to preach the gospel, they endeavoured to force on the Gentile christians the keeping of the law *in the same manner* in which the Jewish christians kept it. This case was referred to the church at Jerusalem with James at their head, and whose decree ought to have been according to our author's division that the Gentiles are free from all the law of Moses, but the Decalogue, but was this the answer *not one word* about the *Decalogue nor one commandment in it,* but after much debate, the following decree was promulgated. " It seems good to the " Holy Ghost and to us, to lay upon you no greater " burthen than these necessary things; that ye abstain " from meats offered to idols and from blood, and " from things strangled, and from fornication: from " which if ye keep yourselves, ye shall do well. Fare " ye well. So when they were dismissed, they came " to Antioch, and when they had gathered the multi- " tude together, they delivered the epistle: which when " they read, they rejoiced for the consolation." And this decree they did not confine to Antioch for it is said in the 4th verse of 16th chapter of Acts, that as they went through the cities they delivered those decrees of the Apostles for them to keep. This case to my mind is demonstrative proof that the Decalogue was never by the Holy Ghost or the Apostles considered separated from the rest of the law, as that portion which the Gentiles had to do with. As to the Jewish christians it is evident, Apostles and all that they kept the ceremonial as well as the moral part of their old

system, and that the keeping it was impressed on them by those very Apostles who exonerated the Gentiles, nay, told them *that their souls " would be subverted"* if they kept these things. Let any one read the following passage. " And the day following Paul went
" in with us unto James; and all the elders were pre-
" sent. And when he had saluted them, he declared
" particularly what things God had wrought among
" the Gentiles by his ministry. And when they had
" heard it, they glorified the Lord, and said unto him,
" Thou seest brother, how many thousands of Jews
" there are which believe; and they are all *zealous of*
" *the law*. And they are informed of thee, that thou
" teachest all the Jews which are among the Gentiles
" *to forsake Moses*, saying, that they ought not to *cir-*
" *cumcise their children, neither to walk after the cus-*
" *toms*. What is it therefore the multitude must needs
" come together: for they will hear that thou art come.
" Do therefore this that we say to thee: We have four
" men which have a vow on them; Them take, and
" *purify thyself with them, and be at charges with*
" *them*, that they may shave their heads: and all may
" know, *that those things, whereof they were informed*
" *concerning thee, are nothing; but that thou thyself*
" *also walkest orderly* AND KEEPEST THE LAW. As
" TOUCHING THE GENTILES which believe we have writ-
" ten and concluded *that they observe no such thing*,
" save only that they keep themselves from things of-
" fered to idols, and from blood, and from things
" strangled, and from fornication. Then *Paul took*
" *the men, and the next day purifying himself* with
" them entered into the temple to signify the accom-

"plishment of the days of purification, until that an "*offering should be offered for every one of them.*" I would here therefore just remark that I never said there was no judaically blending together of the Decalogue, with the precepts of Christ as it related to the *Jewish converts,* but the *Gentiles;* I made this distinction, because I see the Holy Ghost does so; to the Jews, however, there is no separation of the Decalogue from the rest of the Law, (and to those alone do the quotations of our author apply) while they acknowledge any part binding you see them recognizing ceremonial and all, circumcision, sacrifices, vows, &c. &c. And the same remark holds good relative to our Lord's ministry on earth, it was to the lost sheep of the house of Israel. He alone came, till rejected of them; and among them to teach and preach the minutest observance of the law, ceremonial, as well as moral, to pay for cleansing what Moses had commanded, as well as to love the Lord their God with all their heart, with all their soul, and with all their strength, and love their neighbour as themselves; just as in his own person he kept the passover, as he did the Decalogue. The same principle is manifest in all Paul's conduct, for the very same things that he himself did to Jews, or those connected with Judaism, he declared to the Gentiles, if they did, that Christ should profit them nothing, Christ alike commands the young Jew to keep the Decalogue, and the cleansed leper to offer a gift as one come to fulfil and not to break the law, and teach others also, he could not do otherwise, Paul the same, he circumcises Timothy, but refuses to circumcise Titus. From the beginning it is clear the Jewish christians and Gentiles with respect to the measure of the law of Moses to be allowed to them, stood on perfectly different grounds. Our author says, there is no command, but an express prohibition, to keep the ceremonies and rules of the Jews, and the sayings of Christ; with respect to Jewish christians, this is not true, as I have shewn above, and with respect to the Gentiles, our author has not, and cannot, I believe, prove more to have been ever communicated to them as of obligation than those four necessary things to which I have above referred, and which had nothing to do with the decalogue, perhaps it would be well here to consider the passage in 2 Cor. iii. upon which our author makes the following remarks:

"Further, Mr. Groves says, It is precisely of these ten commandments, written on stone, that St. Paul says 'their glory is done away.'" He put the words "their glory is done away" in inverted commas, as if they were a quotation from scripture: but the sagacious reader in vain looks for these words in the cited place 2 Cor. iii. 7, and is surprised to find that it is the glory of Moses' face that is done away! δια την δοξαν τȣ προσωπȣ αυτου την καταλυομενην on acount of the evanescent glory of his, i. e. Mose's face. The thing that was done away, or became evanescent, was the Jewish dispensation called in the 7th verse "the ministration of death" written and engraven in stones; because this dispensation began with the promulgation of the ten commandments on Mount Sinai, which was written in stones. It is very remarkable that the Apostle puts the thing which was evanescent in the neuter gender " το καταργουμενον" i. e. the Jewish dispensation and the thing which was permanent, the gospel dispensation, also in the neuter gender, "το μενον" to indicate the state that was abolished, and the state that remained."

When the Apostle is instituting a comparison between the relative glory of the ministration of death written and engraven on stones, and the ministration of the spirit. The passage runs thus, " Who also hath
" made us able ministers of the New Testament, not
" of the letter, but of the spirit, for the letter killeth,
" but the spirit giveth life. But if the ministration of
" death, written and engraven in stones, was glorious,
" (so that the children of Israel could not steadfastly
" behold the face of Moses for the glory of his counte-
" nance;) which glory was to be done away; how
" shall not the ministration of the spirit be rather glo-
" rious? for if the ministration of condemnation be
" glory, much more doth the ministration of righteous-
" ness exceed in glory. For even that which was made
" glorious had no glory in this respect by reason of the
" glory that excelleth. For if that which was done away
" was glorious, much more that which remaineth is glo-
" rious. Seeing then that we have such hope, we use
" great plainess of speech : and not as Moses, which
" put a veil over his face, that the children of Israel could
" not steadfastly look to the end of that which is abo-
" lished:" (ver. 6—13.) Now let any candid enquirer ask himself what are the things between which a comparison is here instituted, and what respective glories are compared. I think he must say a ministration written and engraven on stones, with a ministration of the Spirit, the ministration of Moses and of Christ and between what is the comparison of glories instituted; but be-

tween the things compared, which surely was not the glory of Moses' face, and the glory of the ministration of the Spirit, but the ministration on stone, with that of the Spirit, and what is predicated respectively of the two; this, namely, that the glory of the one on stone which was to be done away which was abolished (32) had no glory in comparison with that glory which excelleth and remaineth; and concerning the glory of Moses' face, it is evidently only inserted as a measure of the glory of that to be done away, so that if the passage were removed, relative to the glory of Moses' face there would be no hiatus in the sense. Pole in his Synopsis Criticorum, says, it is evident that the moral law was here principally meant as that only was engraven on stones. Bloomfield says in his notes in his Greek Testament on this subject " that the best way
" is to take it *with the ancients* (I believe without ex-
" ception) and some moderns, namely to suppose that
" την καταργουμενην (the being done away) though it
" pertain in appearance to την δοξαν (the glory) in
" fact belongs to γραμματα (writings) meaning the
" Mosaic economy; and that the Apostle meant to
" hint that as that glory was temporary and would
" cease at death, so was the dispensation of whose
" divine origin this was the symbol, meant also to be
" temporary." If I have used therefore the terms
" they are done away" namely the writings, or, as our author says, the dispensation I do so with all the ancients and many moderns, yet surely if the whole

(32) The original here is a forensic word used for the abrogation of a law, and Schleusner says in his remark on the 14th verse that the Mosaic law is abrogated by the christian religion.

dispensation is done away that cannot be excluded which is specified, namely, the decalogue when it is allowed by our author to include that which is not specified, the rest of the dispensation; and indeed our author in the following passage concedes all I desire, when he says, " The thing that was done away (το " καταργουμενον) or became evanescent was the Jewish dispensation, called in the 7th verse " the ministration of death, written and engraven on stones; " because this dispensation began with the promulga- " tion of the *ten commandments on Mount Sinai,* " *which was written on stones* and the το μενον that " which remains means the Gospel." Also in the 7th of the Romans nothing can be more simple than Paul's reasoning, he says, the law must be dead, that law which says, thou shalt not covet, before the church can be married to Him that is risen from the dead without being an adulteress. Also Gal. iv. 21—31. Where the two covenants are compared and declared that they cannot be heirs together. Therefore to any *divine* fixed division of the law into moral, ceremonial and civil, I see not a shadow of evidence, unless I take the author's inferences about mint, anise and cummin, meaning the one and the weightier matters of the law, the other; or some similar conjectural thoughts which are at least sufficiently vague and owing all their weight to his conjectures, not God's declarations which is the thing sought for. And even if this *division* could be fixed as clearly as it cannot, yet I repeat, that the Decalogue had not passed away with the rest of the moral, judicial, and civil law, would have been as far from proved as ever, the contrary would to my mind have appeared certain from our Lord's remarks in Matt. 5 and Paul as quoted above and Jeremiah.

Then to the enquiry, why the tract on the New Testament in the blood of Jesus, was written; I may reply, it never was written, as must have been obvious to the most careless reader, for any, who honestly hold our author's views, these I should not have thought it worth while to have written so largely to disprove, though I should not have thought them true but comparatively harmless, but if our author ever thought his the only views held on this subject the review in the Oriental Spectator must have undeceived him, and it was in reply to this amiable and devoted (yet in my judgment erring brother) my remarks were originally written and those who hold with him; and it was not therefore as our author seems to accuse me (page 29) more than once merely forming a man of straw myself and then demolishing it. The difference between our author and the reviewer in the Oriental Spectator is ten times greater than between him and myself, for this reviewer would leave us at large to wander through the whole law of the Jews, to determine what was to be retained; and at least is an unhappy illustration of what I asserted that there being *no divine authorative division*; every man would be free to divide according to his taste. Our author in one place draws the line, the reviewer in the Oriental Spectator in another, the Roman Catholic in another, each defining what is moral, and to be retained to suit his own system or taste. But though I should not perhaps have ever written a tract against our author's views yet since

I feel persuaded of the impossibility of preventing an amalgamation so displeasing to God when the principle is once conceded, I will endeavour to examine into the question of the decalogue somewhat more at large; and after give a separate consideration to the question of the Sabbath.

Let us then for a moment examine upon what basis the commonly received notion of the Decalogue's being a transcript of the divine mind, or as our Author says " the image of his own eternal divinity" stands. Montesque says that by the laws of a nation you may always judge of its state of morals, and there appears to me great truth in this observation, for laws are promulgated to meet existing vices. The Scripture says, the law was added because of transgression. The contemplation of the mind of God by the Spirit is the grand transforming power in the moral universe of God, whereas, the more you contemplate the Decalogue, the more the thoughts become conversant with the fall of man from God, so far from its being a transcript of God's mind, I question whether those holy beings to whom God's pure mind is ever open, and who dwell in it, would understand the Decalogue, much less discern the Father's likeness there. God's mind was and ever will be, that into which the holy delight to look, the law was not made at all for the righteous to look into, but for the lawless and disobedient, for the ungodly and for sinners, for murderers and whoremongers, liars and perjured persons, &c. &c. not that they may see what God's mind is, but what it hates and has nothing to do with. 1 Tim. 1, 9.—I should therefore rather say, the Decalogue was a transcript of Jehovah's hatred and abhorrence of the idolatrous, adulterous, covetous hearts, of the children of Israel.

JESUS THE TRANSCRIPT OF GOD'S MIND.

How could these prohibitions that have to do only with the lowest and basest sins, that infect a people, be the transcript of a mind that is the perfection of positive good, of LOVE, of which *Christ only is the transcript*. We see the glory of God only shining in the face of Jesus Christ, he alone is the brightness of his Father's glory, and the express image of his person; he alone is the image of the invisible God. It is never said, the Decalogue revealed the Father, but the only begotten Son hath revealed him. Doubtless, as John says the law came by Moses, (33) but grace and truth by Jesus Christ; and therefore the New Testament sets before the Saints of God, not the Ten Commandments, but in the II. Cor. iii. after having shewn the glory of the dispensation on stones, which the Israelites could not look at, but through a veil, he says, referring to the pre-eminent glory of the ministration of the Spirit, " but we all (verse 18.) with open or unveiled face beholding as in a glass, the glory of the Lord, are changed into the same image, from glory to glory as by the spirit of the Lord—Can any Gentile then, without a warrant from Scripture, look to these moral elements for a rule, or light, rather than to Jesus—My full conviction is, that Paul meant what he said in the widest sense, when he declared the Law made *nothing* perfect; the Deca-

(33) Our Author asks why I use the appellation " Moses' law" and not the "law of God" my answer is because the Holy Ghost has so done in the New Testament with hardly an exception when referring to this law. Christ always says Moses law and your law See John 1. 17, 45.—7, 19, 23.—6, 5,—15, 25.—18, 31.—Acts 13, 39, 15, 5.—Heb. 9, 19.—10, 28.

logue in its department, as the ceremonial and judicial in theirs, all had reference to the hardness of heart and low state of feeling of the people generally, yet in those times glorious if compared with any thing but the manifestation of the Father in the face of Jesus Christ, but in comparison with this, all as Paul says, beggarly rudiments; and my strongest objection to our author's view after considering it as being dishonorable to Jesus, is that the holding of the Decalogue as a Rule of Life, and a perfect rule of life is the fruitful source of all that *negative* religion which prevails, naming some few gross sins which we are NOT to commit, and which the great mass of individuals find it no difficult matter to convince themselves they do not commit, instead of that perfect Jesus, as I have before observed, who so convinces all who profess his name with any measure of honesty, of their short comings, that none can persuade themselves that they do keep his precepts; and most endeavour to prove like the Jew in Justin Martyr, that they are too perfect to be kept; and this is proved by the answer to our Lord of him, who said all these have I kept from my youth up. Paul could say as touching the righteousness which is of the law blameless, Zechariah and Elizabeth walked in all the ordinances of the law blameless. Who ever yet felt he had kept all the commandments of Jesus from his youth, or had kept them without blame. The great peculiarity of the Decalogue, as compared with the precepts of Jesus as a rule of life, is this, to convict any one by the Decalogue of a breach of it, allowing it the amplitude its advocates claim for it, you must in 99 cases out of a hundred, exceed the letter, for any one to escape under the new Testament, you must deny the possibility of carrying out the strictness of the letter. And you see it in all pamphlets on this subject, the advocates of the Decalogue endeavour to prove it means *more* than it says, and when they turn round to the New Testament, when they come to the plainest precepts and examples to self devotion to the Lord, they seek to prove these mean less than they say. I shall have an opportunity of shewing this more strikingly, when I institute at some length a comparison between our authors proposed perfect rule of life, and that which the Lord Jesus by himself or his Apostles has delivered as the rule of life, to the Gentile Church.

IMPORTANCE OF A DEFINITE RULE OF LIFE.

Nothing can certainly be of more importance to man as a religious being, than to have such a rule of life, as prevents him on the one hand judging as evil, actions that are holy, or following as holy, actions that violate the will of God. It is very true, that those who like our author, contend only for the reservation of the Decalogue, may *comparatively* easily be dealt with but may not the reviewer in the *Oriental Spectator* have his view of what is to be retained, since the Scripture makes no authoritative division, as I have shewn, and thus he does divide, or confound the dispensation of real humiliation, with that of typical glory and with this mixed seed sows his field. It is also very convenient to the slave holder to take another part, to the polygamist another, and thus they destroy the unity and beauty of the present dispensation, for our authors declaration must not be forgotten, that all Gods legislations harmonise, therefore none of Gods Laws or Acts whether contained in the Decalogue or elsewhere, could be against the immutable morality of the Decalogue, and therefore polygamy, slavery, concubinage, cannot as our author wishes, be considered the glosses of the Pharisees, David's Polygamy was Gods own act, he having done it, it never could be any thing but holy, and in accordance with the meaning and intention of the Decalogue, for as our author states " God never made one law to contradict another" or in other words, whatever any statute or judgment in all the Sinai covenant allowed, was in unison with the meaning of the Decalogue, otherwise the laws would contradict each other, indeed, when the Decalogue is called a summary of the law, does it not imply its full meaning must be sought for in the more expanded. What our author says may be true, that if men want to do their own will, they will not fail to find an excuse, yet this does not exonerate us from being able to shew Satan or his servants, where the thing they would have done is forbidden, or that which they would forbid is commanded. " It is written" silenced Satan, and may and will his boldest servant. But again let us examine the assertion made that the Decalogue is needed as a rule of life, and is in fact a perfect rule, and that by which we can alone convict of sin.

The grand argument in favor of the convicting power of the law, is from what Paul says in the 7th of the Romans, surely had our author honestly dealt with this whole argument, he would have in the first place pointed out what Paul was arguing about, Paul had been saying that the Jewish Church would have been an adulteress in being married to Christ, had not the law been dead that bound her to her former husband. But when he had in the 6th Verse declared his deliverance from the law previous to his new marriage, he meets the question supposed to be put to him. Is then the law sin? By the reply, I had not known sin, but by the law, for I had not known lust ; except the law (ονομος) had said thou shalt not covet, but Paul says the commandment (εντολη) also was holy, just and good which according to our authors criticism as I have before observed on its Hebrew synonyme, is distinguished from the moral law, and refers to the ceremonial and Judicial parts of the law, and corresponds to the Hebrew word חק (34) which he declares (page 22) to mean " statute" and to be one of those words in whose use (in this restricted sense) there is a very *remarkable distinction, and deserving the most serious notice as clearly indicating the intention of the Holy Spirit, relative to that law which is holy, just, and good, in contradistinction to*

(34) If any one wishes to see the use of either the Greek word εντολη or the Hebrew חק let him consult Taylor's Hebrew Concordance or Trommius's Greek Concordance of the Sept. or Schmidt's Conc. of the Greek N. T. where he will see that it is used in reference to commands of every kind.

that which was to pass away; whereas in his criticism, page 42, on this very word, he declares it to mean the separate precepts of the Decalogue, in which of the two interpretations, our author is right, I do not here stop to enquire, yet all I see worthy the most serious notice is, that he cannot be right in both his criticisms. Yes both the law and commandments of the first husband were holy, just, and good, he does not wish to speak evil of either, whilst he declares they were now dead to him; and as he said in II. Cor. Glorious as they were, they had no glory in comparison with that which remaineth and excelleth, the law of the spirit of life of his new husband; this we contend with Paul is more glorious, holier, and better, and in comparison with which, the others were but meagre rudiments." And surely it is a most absurd principle to lay down that because Paul asserts, that the law of his old husband, convicted him of *one* sin which he *specifies*, that therefore it would convict of *all sins* which *he does not specify*; and that all the multiplied rules in the New Testament, about the same sin and its character and consequences, *could not* convict of sin without its aid, this is indeed arguing from a particular to a general in the first case, and in opposition to reason and experience in the second. Does Paul say that on being married to the new husband the risen Lord of Glory, the bride has to go to her old dead husband for a rule of life, rather than her new and living Head, the Father's only begotten Son, it may have been allowed to her weakness but not enjoined on her faith, there appears to me indeed something so monstrous and unnatural in the very supposition, that Christ should *direct* his Jewish members even to look back to their dead husband for their rule of life, rather than to himself the risen Lord of Glory, how infinitely more so the Gentile bride, who never was another's but married as a " chaste virgin" to Christ! it so outrages all analogies. And though it could be proved as I think it cannot, that the rule in the Decalogue or whole Sinai Covenant, was as perfect as the New Testament rule, still to direct the bride of Christ to look back upon Moses whom Paul was so anxious to marry, as I have observed, to *one Husband* as a *chaste Virgin*, and that Husband Christ, would be like directing a wife to walk by the rule of her dead and not her living husband, as it regards the Jew, and to the Gentile, it would be as directing a bride to walk by the rule of another's husband, the very habit of looking to the will of another, would vitiate and corrupt all the beauty and chastity of their new relations, even though the acts separately considered, might be all her husband could desire, all their preciousness would have vanished, which would consist only in this, that they were done to him and for him.

RULES OF LIFE COMPARED.

In order, however, that the *uselessness* of this may also fully appear, I perhaps could not choose a better place than this, to institute the comparison between the rule proposed by our author and that by myself, for although he admits the appending the New Testament precepts to the Decalogue still as a rule of life, or for conviction of sin, he declares the Decalogue to be perfect and so essential to all holy walk, that he who takes only the New Testament Rule, illuminated by the example of Jesus and the Apostles is a lawless one, an Antinomian, whereas, I have over and over again asked my opponents, to point out one unholy action the New Testament alone would allow, or one holy one it does not enjoin, I shall now proceed to shew, had I been so challenged, to prove the insufficiency of the Decalogue, that I should not have remained long without giving an answer, and shewing a pretty extended catalogue of deficiencies, I shall proceed 1st by shewing how far the New Testament alone supplies a rule of life, parallel to those in the Decalogue, and then proceed to show how far it extends beyond all that the Decalogue at all events declares, and I believe even contemplated.

DECALOGUE RULE OF LIFE.	NEW TESTAMENT RULE OF LIFE.
Motives to obedience under the law.	Motives of obedience under the Gospel.
I am the Lord thy God, which brought thee out of the land of Egypt, out of the house of bondage.	God commended his love *towards us* in that while we were yet sinners Christ died for us.
	Herein is love, not that we loved God, but that He loved us, and sent His Son to be the propitiation for our sins. I. John iv., 10, see also iii. 1, 2.
	Who hath delivered us from the power of darkness and translated us into the Kingdom of his dear Son, Col. i. 13.

I.

Thou shalt have none other Gods than me.

I.

To us there is but one God the Father, of whom are all things, and we in Him, and one Lord Jesus Christ by whom are all things, and we by Him. I. Cor. viii. 6.

We know that the Son of God is come, and hath given us understanding that we should know Him that is true, and we are in Him that is in His Son Jesus Christ—this (person) is the true God and eternal life. I. John v. 20.

II.

Thou shalt not make unto thee any graven image, or any likeness of any thing that is in Heaven above, or that is in the earth beneath, or that is in the water under the earth.

Thou shalt not bow down thyself to them nor serve them. For I the Lord thy God am a jealous God, visiting the iniquity of the Fathers upon the Children into the 3rd and 4th generation of them that hate me, and shewing mercy unto thousands of them that love me

II.

God is a spirit, and they that worship Him must worship Him in spirit and in truth. John iv. 24.

Little Children keep yourselves from Idols. I. John v. 21.

Wherefore my dearly beloved flee from Idolatry. I. Cor. x. 12.

If any man that is called a brother be an Idolater, with such an one no not to eat. I. Cor. v. 11.

Mortify your members which are on the earth, coveteousness which is Idola-

and keep my commandments.

III.

Thou shalt not take the name of the Lord thy God in vain; for the Lord wilt not hold him guiltless that taketh his name in vain.

try. Cor. iii. 5, the works of the flesh which are manifest are these, Idolatry, Witchcraft. Gal. v. 19, 20.

III.

Swear not at all, neither by Heaven, for it is Gods throne; nor by the earth, for it is his footstool. Mat. v. 34, 35.

He that shall swear by Heaven, sweareth by the throne of God and by Him that sitteth thereon. Mat. xxiii. 22. Let your communications be yea, yea, and nay, nay, for whatsoever is more than these cometh of evil Mat. v. 37. But above all things my brethren swear not, neither by heaven, neither by the earth, neither by *any other oath*: but let your yea be yea, and your nay, nay; lest ye fall into condemnation.

IV.

Remember the Sabbath-day to keep it holy. Six days shall thou labour and do all thy work.

But the seventh day is the Sabbath of the Lord thy God: in it thou shalt do no manner of work thou nor thy son nor thy daughter,

IV.

The Son of man is Lord also of the Sabbath. Luke vi. 5. The Sabbath was made for man and not man for the Sabbath. Mark ii. 29.

Let no man therefore judge you in meat, or in drink, or in respect of an holyday, or of the new moon, thy man-servant nor thy maid-servant, nor thy cattle nor thy stranger that is within thy gate. For in six days the Lord made Heaven and Earth, the Sea and all that in them is, and rested the seventh day and hallowed it.

or of the *Sabbath*, which are a shadow of things to come but the body is of Christ. Col. ii. 16, 17.

V.

Honor thy Father and thy Mother, that thy days may be long upon the land which the Lord thy God giveth thee.

V.

Children obey your Parents in the Lord for this is right, honor your Father and Mother which is the 1st Commandment with promise. Eph. vi. 1, 2.

Children obey your Parents in all things, for this is well pleasing unto the Lord. Col. iii. 20.

VI.

Thou shalt do no murder.

VI.

We have heard that it hath been said to them of old time, thou shalt not kill, and whosoever shall kill shall be in danger of the Judgment, but I say unto you that whosoever is angry with his brother without cause, shall be in danger of the Judgment. Mat. v. 21, 22.

Murderers shall have their portion in the lake that burneth with fire and brimstone. Rev. xxi. 8.

He that hateth his brother is a murderer, and ye know that no murderer hath eternal life abiding in Him. I. John iii. 8.

Without (the city) are murderers. Rev. xxii. 15.

VII.
Thou shalt not commit adultery.

VII.
Ye have heard that it hath been said to them of old time, thou shalt not commit adultery but I say unto you, that whosoever looketh on a woman to lust after her, hath committed adultery already with her in his heart. Mat. v. 27, 28.

Out of the heart proceed evil thoughts, adulteries—these are the things that defile the man. Mat. xv. 19, 20.

Adultery a work of the flesh. Gal. v. 19.

Adulterers God will judge. Heb. xiii. 4.

Adulterers shall not inherit the kingdom of God. I. Cor. vi. 9. II. Peter ii. 13, 14. Rom. xiii. 9.

VIII.
Thou shalt not steal.

VIII.
Let him that stole steal no more, but rather let him

| IX.
Thou shalt not bear false witness against thy neighbour. | labour working with his hands, that he may have to give to him that needeth. Eph. iv. 28.

Thieves shall not inherit the Kingdom of God. I. Cor. vi. 10.

IX.
Thou shalt not bear false witness. Rom. xiii. 9.

False witness proceeds from the heart and defiles a man. Mat. xv. 19.

Without are dogs, and every one that loveth and maketh a lie. Rev. xxii. 15. |

X.
Thou shalt not covet thy neighbours house, thou shalt not covet thy neighbours wife, nor his manservant, nor his maidservant, nor his ox, nor his ass, nor any thing that is thy neighbours.

X.
Coveteousness let it not be once named among you as becometh Saints. Eph. v. 3.

Let your conversation be without coveteousness. Heb. xiii. 15.

Thou shalt not covet. Rom. xiii. 9.

Mortify coveteousness which is idolatry. Col. iii. 5.

If any man that is called a brother be covetous with such an one, no not to eat. I. Cor. v. 22.

The covetous shall not inherit the kingdom of God. I. Cor. vi. 10.

Here then I trust I have sufficiently clearly shewn, that the new Testament gives far fuller directions on most of these points, than the Decalogue which is considered essential to convict men of sin by, and here it must be remembered our author with myself, means only *instrumentally*, for he fully acknowledges that the Holy Spirit alone can bring any sin home on the conscience as a sin against God, however perfect the rule may be. The Sabbath is the only point on which in the New Testament gives no other directions, than those given by the Apostle of the Gentiles, who declares we are not to be judged about it, because it was only a shadow which had found its fulfilment in Christ, and which we enter into the enjoyment and possession of as we do of every other shadow, by realizing the substance of it in Christ by faith and in fact every mention of regard to days, is named as a circumstance to excite alarm not emulation; our Lord prepared the way to this doing away of the Sabbath as a shadow, by declaring himself first the Lord of it, here lies his legislative right to do it away and Paul says he was the substance of it shewing its end. Paul says generally concerning days, one man esteemeth one day better than another, another esteemeth every day alike; let every man be fully persuaded in his own mind, this our author thinks refers to days exclusive of the Lord's day, but I think the contrary, and for this reason, that when the Apostle is referring to the keeping of these other Jewish days, he disallows them to the Gentiles. For concerning these when writing to the Galatians, he says, ye observe days, and times, and years, *I am afraid* of you lest I have bestowed upon you labour in vain, here is no allowance as in the other case, for each man to do as he was persuaded was best, but a declaration that if they kept those Jewish festivals, they vitiated their Christian position, so as to allow him little hope of their state.

I would here again remark—Secondly, that the sanctions are only two, by which the authority of the Decalogue is upheld, the one was being cast off the land that God had given them for dishonoring their parents, the other that their children for three or four generations, should suffer the effects of their fathers sins, if they became idolaters, and that, the Lord would shew mercy unto thousands that love him and keep his commandments. Whilst the breaches of these laws in the New Testament are declared not to exclude from dwelling in the earth in prosperity, (which is in the New Testament rather a promise to the godly to be served as Christ was,) but to be excluded from the Kingdom of Heaven, to be cast into the lake that burneth for ever and ever, to be where the worm dieth not and the fire is not quenched, now I would ask any one which would serve as the most powerful auxiliary to one preaching the gospel of the Grace of God and entreating men to flee from the wrath to come; or when pointing men to the grace that has provided a way to escape from the fearful looking for of judgment and fiery indignation, that shall finally consume the adversaries? Or when seeking to give them any adequate notion of the exceeding sinfulness of sin even in these few and gross particulars which would be most efficient; referring them to a Decalogue which denounces nothing but temporal sufferings to themselves, or their posterity on the breach of two of its commands and a simple prohibition without any threat of punishment immediate, or remote, on the breach of all the other eight, or referring him to a revelation where every feeling of the heart is arrested, by the most appalling considerations of interminable sorrows, or the most glowing and alluring exhibitions of everlasting glory, to be the respective portions of the sinners and the saints in that day, when the earth and its glory shall vanish, the loftiness of man be brought down, and the Lord alone exalted, as King of kings, and Lord of lords. But I will now proceed to consider the efficiency of the New Testament as a rule of life in the two grand points both of conviction of sin, and instruction in righteousness, in matters concerning which the Decalogue gives no light.

A summary of some of the grosser sins against which the Decalogue furnishes no rule, but which the New Testament forbids and awfully condemns.

DRUNKARDS.

Be not drunk with wine, but be filled with the Spirit. Eph. v. 10. If any man called a brother, be a drunkard, with such an one, no not to eat. 1 Cor. v. 11. Drunkards shall not inherit the Kingdom of God. 1 Cor. vi. 10.

LIARS.

Lie not one to another seeing ye have put off the old man and his lusts. Col. iii. 9. Putting away lying. Eph. iv. 25. All liars shall have their portion in the lake that burneth with fire and brimstone. Rev. xxi. 8.

EXTORTIONERS.

If any man called a brother be an extortioner, with such an one no not to eat. 1 Cor. vii. also Mat. xxii. 35.

FORNICATORS.

Fornications come from within and defile the man. Mark vii. 21, 23. The body is not for fornication but for the Lord. 1, Cor. vi. 13. Flee fornication. 1 Cor. vi. 13. Gal. v. 19. If any that is called a brother, be a fornicator with such an one no not to eat. 1 Cor. v. 11, also Heb. xii. 16.

WHOREMONGERS.

Whoremongers, God will judge. Heb. xiii. 4. Whoremongers shall have their part in the lake that burneth with fire. Rev. xxi. 8. No whoremonger hath any inheritance in the kingdom of Christ. Eph. v. 5. Without are whoremongers. Rev. xxii. 15.

Some of those sins not forbidden in the Decalogue on which the utmost stress is laid in the gospel as the instrument of reproof and conviction of sin. The righteousness of God however is specially manifested in the Gospel by the nature of those precepts given to men for instruction in righteousness.

For Conviction of Sin.	For Instruction in Righteousness.
The spirit shall convince the world of sin, because they	Herein (i. e. In the Gospel) the righteousness of God

believe not on me, John xvi. 8, 9. He that believeth not is condemned already, because he hath not believed in the name of the only begotten son of God. John. He that believeth not shall be damned. The fearful and unbelieving shall have their portion in the lake. Rev. xxi. 8. Whatsoever is not of faith is sin.

is revealed from faith to faith, as it is written, the just shall live by faith. He that believeth shall be saved, believe in the Lord Jesus Christ and thou shall be saved. Acts. He that believeth in Him is not condemned, without faith it is impossible to please God. Heb. xi. 16. Fight the good fight of faith.

MALICE, ENVY, &c.

Werefore, laying aside all malice and all guile and hypocrisies and envies and all evil speakings, I. Pet. ii. 1. Let us walk not in strife and envying Rom. xiii. 13. Cor. iii. 3. By nature we all live in malice and envy. James iv. 5. Tit. iii. 8.

MEEKNESS, GENTLENESS, LOVE, &c.

As new born babes desire the sincere milk of the word that we may grow thereby. I. Pet. ii. 1. Put on therefore as the elect of God, holy and beloved, bowels of mercies, kindness, humbleness of mind, meekness, long suffering. Col. iii. 12, 13.

WORKS OF THE FLESH.

The works of the flesh are hatred, variance, emulations, wrath, strife, seditions, sects, of the which I tell you before as I have told you in times past, that they who do such things shall not inherit the kingdom of God. Gal. v. 20.

WORKS OF THE SPIRIT.

But the fruit of the Spirit is love, joy, peace, long-suffering, gentleness, goodness, faith, meekness, temperance. Gal. v. 22, 23.

But the wisdom which is from above is first pure, then peaceable, gentle, and easy to

21. Where envy and strife is, there is confusion and every evil work. This wisdom descendeth not from above but *is* earthly, sensual, devilish. James. iii.14 to 17.

be entreated, full of mercy and good fruits without wrangling and without hypocrisy.

Foolish Talking.

Foolish talking and jestings which are not convenient, let it not be once named among you as becometh saints. Eph. v 3.4. For every idle word that men shall speak they shall give account thereof in the day of Judgement. Mat. xii. 36. By thy words thou shall be condemned. xii. 37.

Holy Converse.

James iii. 17. But rather giving of thanks, speaking to yourselves in Psalms and Hymns and Spiritual songs—speak every man truth with his neighbour and speaking the truth in love. Eph. iv. 15, 25. Exhort one another daily. Heb. iii. 13. Comfort edify and admonish one another. I. Tim. v. 11. Rom. xvi. 19. xv. 4. By thy words thou shalt be justified. Mat. xii. 37. Whatever you do in word or deed, do all to the Glory of God.

Pride.

Pride cometh from within and defiles a man, Mark vii. 22. God resisteth the proud, I. Pet. v. 5. He hath scattered the proud in the imaginations of their heart. Luke 1. *51*

Humility.

Be clothed with humility. God giveth grace unto the humble. *Humble* yourselves in the sight of the Lord and he will lift you up. Let this mind be in you, which was also in Christ Jesus. Read Ph. ii. 11.

LOVE OF THE WORLD CONDEMNED.	DYING TO THE WORLD ENJOINED.
Keep yourselves unspotted from the world. James 1. 27.	I die daily. I. Cor. xv. 31. By the Cross of the Lord Jesus the world is crucified unto me and I unto the world. Gal. vi. 14. He that hateth his life in this world shall save it unto life eternal. John xii. 25.
If any man love the world, the love of the Father is not in him. 1. John. II. 15.	
Ye adulterers and adultresses know ye not that the friendship of the world is enmity with God. James iv. 4.	
All that is in the world, the lust of the flesh, the lust of the eye, and the pride of life, is not of the Father, but of the world. I. John ii. 16.	

The duties also of Husbands, Wives, Masters, Servants and Subjects, though not forming any part of the Decalogue, are not only legislated for by the Gospel, but have likewise a sacredness and importance given them they never had before, being urged upon such high and exalted motives, that of adorning the doctrine of God our Saviour in all things, being followers of God as dear children and walking, worthy of the vocation wherewith we are called.

HUSBANDS.

Husbands love your wives even as Christ loved the Church, Ep. v. 22 to 24. Col. iii. 19. I. Peter iii. 7.

WIVES.

Wives submit yourselves unto your own husbands as unto the Lord, Eph. v. 22-24. Col. iii. 18. See also the *minute* directions concerning the conduct of married women. I. Peter iii. 1-6.

Masters.

Masters give your servants that which is just and equal, knowing that we also have a Master in Heaven. Col. iv. 1.

Servants.

Servants obey in all things your Masters according to the flesh, not with eye service, as men pleasers, but in singleness of heart fearing God. Col. iii. 22 to 25, I. Tim. vi. 1-3. Tit. ii. 9, 10. I. Pet. ii. 18, 9.

Subjects.

I exhort that first of all, supplication, prayers, intercessions and giving of thanks be made for all men: for kings and for all that are in authority. I. Tim. ii. 1 to 3.

Render unto Cæsar the things that are Cæsar's. Mat. xxii. 21. Luke xx. 25.

Let every soul be subject unto the higher powers, for there is no power but of God, the powers that be are ordained of God. Rom. xiii. 1-7.

Submit yourselves to every ordinance of man for the Lord's sake. I. Pet. ii. 13-17. Titus iii. 1.

The sacredness and importance of these relations in life, consist as will be seen by the text, from their involving in their carrying out, principles, aims and objects, which at once purifies, dignifies and exalts them. A husband and a wife are to represent, or shadow forth the love Christ bears his Church—and the duty the Church owes her head, servants, or slaves—are, to serve not as men-pleasers but in singleness of heart fearing God—and subjects recognize the powers that be, as ordained of God—and therefore learn for the Lord's sake to submit to every ordinance of man.

CONCLUDING REMARKS.

I fear to lengthen the catalogue or could add very many precepts on most important subjects not provided for in the Decalogue, such as the duty of caring for the poor, needy, and afflicted, JAMES. And keeping ourselves unspotted from the world—the duty of loving each other *as Christ has loved us*—being ready to lay down our lives for a brother.

Duties of the rich to sell all and give to the poor, being contented with food and raiment—and of the poor to be content with such things that they have; knowing that God hath said, He will never leave nor forsake them—Lastly, the duty of taking up our Cross daily, bearing all things, enduring all things—taking it patiently, if when we do well we suffer for it, knowing we are thereunto called, seeing Christ left us an example that we should follow his steps.

At the close of this most imperfect summary of a few striking particular and general rules of life for believers from the New Testament, contrasted with and amplified as they evidently are beyond all comparison above the prohibitory rules against the most open and sensual sins with which the Decalogue has almost alone to do, I cannot but confess that the charges of Antinomianism attempted to be set up surprises and grieves me, had I observed an attempt, however unsuccessful to found upon this contested point, a purer, more exalted rule of spiritual service, than that which I had maintained, a more full and unreserved obedience to the whole will of God, or a struggle for the dedication of themselves and all they possessed more entirely to God, I should have respected their zeal, however, I might question its wisdom, but from any thing I have ever seen of the results of the zeal of any on this question, I feel utterly unable to allow any spiritual reason for the necessity of retaining the Decalogue as a rule of life, being urged on the ground of the lawless position of those who have it not, and if the zeal of those who urge it was a holy zeal for the interests of morals, it would equally strive to see every part of the will of God more extensively and effectually carried out, but as it is it has to my mind much of the air of hypocrisy in it; what my heart has longed to see is this zeal extended over the appropriation of the other six days to God, to redeem every time, every portion of the silver, of the gold, and consecrating it to Him, when I see this though I may still think it a zeal without knowledge, I shall be fully prepared to allow its honesty. But I believe were the true reasons stated of this zeal, one of the strongest would be found to be, because it gives the only apparent *divine* precept to support those claims made by Protestant professional teachers of religion, on the time of their hearers on that day; the Roman Catholics, and the

English Establishment after they had separated from the Papacy, retained too much of the notion of the power of the keys possessed by them, to loose or bind respecting all such matters, to regard the question and felt no particular need of pressing this principle, but many of the other reformers and Puritans who wished to stand by the *professed* Protestant watchword " the Bible and nothing but the Bible" felt that if they cast away all days of man's institution, they were in danger of having no day at all for the discharge of their official duties, at least that they could lay claim to on grounds sufficiently commanding, they contended therefore for the appropriation of the Decalogue, as the immutable moral law of God against the Papists and English Establishment, as we see by the resistance of the Puritans to Charles's book of sports, and the Puritans and all who wished to attack their licentious use of the Lord's day, finding the New Testament afforded them little specific ground for denouncing their opponents they assumed for this purpose the right to use the Decalogue as the battle axe, to the end that they might be able to bring the Old Testament denunciations on the breach of the observance of that day, to bear upon their disorderly adversaries. having their thoughts with respect to times just where the woman of Sychar had her's with respect to places, fancying some peculiar holiness attached to the one or the other to Garizim or Jerusalem, when the Lord taught her that the coming dispensation should know nothing of places, just as the whole new Testament knows nothing in its legislation of times, but contemplates the redemption Christ has wrought, to be of every place as a sanctuary of God, and every time in the midst of every occupation, as a day of holy convocation to the Lord, " whatever you do, do all to the glory of God," sanctifies every occupation, every season and every place, and turns the whole life into one day of holy worship, and this is what the natural heart hates and to which the renewed heart, but slowly is brought to delight in, one day as a tribute to God to redeem the use of the rest of our time to ourselves, one-tenth of our property to redeem the use of the rest to our pleasures is most pleasant to the mind, that wishes to unite the earth, and heaven together, but to make every hour and every occupation the silver and the gold the Lord's without limitation or reserve, (and this alone is the gospel rule of life) is what the indwelling of Jesus alone by the Spirit can make any son of Adam love, or be obedient to.

ON THE SABBATH.

I believe no one will deny that our true wisdom is to fall in with the designs of God in his government of the universe, and that the great end of all religion is not mere activity in any present outward ordinances, but in seeking to find out God's design in them, this alone will enable us in complicated circumstances to act with steadiness or peace. For instance, Moses who saw through all his circumstances in Egypt, up to the time when that greater Prophet was to be raised up like unto him, to whom the people were to give ear, was enabled the moment the glory of Egypt, was presented on the one hand, and the reproach of Christ on the other to choose rather the suffering affliction with the people of God than to enjoy the pleasure of sin for a season. What was it then that made this holy and blessed man so wise above those around him, it was that he saw Christ as the end, and that he had fellowship with the Son of God in his sufferings, and saw the moral glory of them, and therefore he endured as seeing him who was as yet invisible but to faith, and thus he lived in the end with Christ, and what is it that now makes so many look to him, who himself looked up to Jesus, it is that fellowship in the sufferings of Jesus has no charms for them for they see not God's end in them but the pleasures and profits of the world have, and these ends being proposed to sense they seize on them. Let us again look at Abraham, what was it that made him content to be a pilgrim and wanderer, it was that he saw Christ's day and was glad that he looked for a City, that had foundations whose maker and builder was God, and when he might have returned to the City, out of which he came he would not, being cheered on his way by this hope, still the eye of hope in all was on Christ, here was to them the light of life, the faith that made them overcome the world. A man in Noah's time who saw God's end in any dispensation or part of a dispensation lived in its end, and those who though living in the times of the end, do not discern God's design grope as blindmen at noon day. And this is the very charge that Paul in the 2 Cor. iii. brings against the followers of Moses, that they could not see the *end* of that which was abolished, the glory of that put out their eyes, so that Moses required a veil which veil is taken away says Paul in Christ. From the earliest to the latest event in Scripture whoever pursues it not up to its due position with Christ, stops short of its real end and his instruction and sanctification; and in proportion to his ignorance about the real end proposed, will be his bigotry and bitterness about the means. Now this principle pre-eminently applies to the discussion of the Sabbath, and we shall see this in the conduct of all the Jews relative to their controversies with our Lord on this subject they saw not Gods design in the Sabbath but looking upon it as something holy to keep in the way prescribed, *not as a shadow*, but a *substance*. The first enquiry of every Jew and sabbatizing Christian therefore ought to be what *end* did God propose in the institution of the sabbath. Our author tells us, its morality consists in this, that man owes a certain portion of his time to God, to this, all that can be said is that it is a mere fancy, unsupported by any allusion in scripture, and contrary to the plainest reasons which God has assigned for its institution or description of its nature, and indeed had it been this as it would have been immaterial what day in the seven it was, so also it would have been immaterial whether it was a seventh of each day or one day in seven. But really rest* and not service was its peculiarity, therefore there was no specific worship enjoined on that day to the people in the Decalogue, nor punishment for

* See Ap: A.

not worshipping, though there was for not resting. But to shew that it typified a boon from God to be realized by faith and not a service to be paid to Him, let us read Heb. iv 1—11. where the apostle says " Let us therefore fear, lest a promise being left us of entering into his rest, any of you should seem to come short of it. For unto us was the gospel preached, as well as unto them, but the word preached did not profit them, not being mixed with faith in them that heard it. For we which *have believed* DO *enter into rest;* as he said, as I have sworn in my wrath, if they should enter into my rest: although the works were finished from the foundation of the world. For he spoke in a certain place of the seventh day on this wise, and God did rest the seventh day from all his works, and in this place again, if they shall enter into my rest seeing therefore it remaineth that some must enter therein, and they to whom it was first preached entered not in because of unbelief: (Again he limiteth a certain day, saying in David, to-day, after so long a time; as it is said, to-day if he will hear his voice, harden not your hearts. For if Jesus had given them rest, then would he not afterward have spoken of another day. There remaineth therefore a rest to the people of God. For he that is entered into his rest, he also hath ceased from his own works, as God did from his.) Let us labour therefore to enter into the rest, lest any man fall after the same example of unbelief." The whole idea here is a favour received from God, not a duty or service to be paid to him, and only by faith to be possessed: let the author of the Perpetuity bring one text to prove that the Sabbath was required as a *debt* man owed to God, and as such was required of him; it is very true the ransomed child of God owes all time, all talents, all the capabilities of every situation to him who has redeemed him, as Paul says not to live unto himself but to him, who died for him, and rose again, but the essential character of service is activity, whilst that of the sabbath is rest, what then does the Sabbath signify it is a day of which Christ says he is the Lord, here again you see the one object of all ordinances, but more Paul in Colossians (35) says it was a shadow of which Christ was the body. Here then the scriptures and our author are at direct variance, he says, that its holiness essentially lies in this, that man owes a portion of his time to God and therefore it is essentially holy in the nature of things. Paul says it is a shadow of which Christ is the body. I shall leave our author to shew how on his system Christ is the body, and proceed to shew how scripture brings it out. Let us remember these things are clear from God's word, that Christ is the Lord of the Sabbath, and also the body of the Sabbath. The author says, page 63, in a quotation, the duty of observing a Sabbath must continue as long as the type exists. "*That is while time lasts,*" now I will take it for granted, that our author would allow that shadow and substance, and type and antitype are

---

(35) The Greek here is plural, but this is of no consequence, as we shall see by referring to the following passages where though the noun be plural, the meaning is indisputably singular. Matthew 12, 1, 11, 28 : 1. Mark 1, 21. 2, 23. 24 x 3, 2. Luke 4, 16 x 13 10 Acts 13, 14. and our author allows it is included. (See Appendix A.)

similar relations, and therefore, that I may say if the body is come the shadow is done away, as truly as if the antitype is come, the type is done away. If so then the shadow of a Sabbath is done away by the coming of the body Christ Jesus and that the thing designed in the perfect rest of the Sabbath had nothing whatever to do with time devoted to God as a debt, therefore particular service or worship as I have observed is no where enjoined as a part of the mode of keeping it, it was simple bodily rest, and this typified the rest the soul was to enter into that believed (Heb. iv.) in Jesus, the perfection of the rest of body shadowed forth the perfection of the rest of soul, and therefore Christ says, come unto me all ye that labour and are heavy laden and I will give you rest. Take my yoke upon you and learn of me, for I am meek and lowly of heart, and ye shall find rest unto your souls. And Paul says in the Hebrews, we who believe do enter into rest, the *old rest* of the *body* in the sabbath, shadowed forth Christ as the *body* of the souls true rest. From the first institution of the Sabbath it shadowed forth Christ its true body, and whosoever has seen this end in the Sabbath has used it to God and he would see how fit it was that there should be absolute cessation from our own works to shadow forth the perfection of that rest which Christ was to bring the soul and the examination of my soul now as to its keeping a Sabbath according to the will of God would have nothing to do with an enquiry into the strictness of bodily rest one day in seven, but whether I was living in the constant enjoyment of that rest of spirit and peace of soul in Jesus through faith in his finished work of the new creation; whether I had really become a new creature, old things having passed away and all things having become new, if so faith has put my soul into the possession of the substance of the sabbath and it would be as completely sapping the foundations of the gospel to preach and enjoin bodily rest *as such* on the Church of Christ as circumcision or sacrifices, for the Sabbath, circumcision, and sacrifices, were alike shadows and instituted to shew forth the body Christ, and which were all alike done away for ever when the substance came, and Christ by his sacrifice and resurrection put an end to sacrifices and sin and became the true and abiding rest of his people, and which now can only be enjoyed as Paul (Heb. iv.) shews by faith or forfeited by unbelief. You may as well argue for the continuance of sacrifices when the true Lamb is come as for the keeping of a Sabbath when the true Sabbath or rest is come. Our Lord's day is now rightly used not when our hearts are thinking about bodily rest, but when we remember Christ our very Paschal *Lamb* and Christ the true rest of our souls through faith, and on these foundations worship him in the beauty of holiness, according therefore to what scripture says of the design both of sacrifices, circumcision, and the sabbath, I should expect to see neither the one nor the other mentioned, but as having found their fulfilment in Christ and this is precisely the place I find them occupy in the new Testament only alluded to as shadows, the body of which was come, and nothing but this could I think make me understand how the observance of the Sabbath should never have been alluded to as an ordinance in all the Apostolic writings.

I know it may be asked does not the sabbath typify the rest of heaven, if you mean by it the rest of the inheritance of heaven. I answer no where that I know of in scripture, Canaan is a type of the heavenly LAND of rest, but the sabbath day was a type of the *nature* of the rest of the inhabitants in that land which is the souls rest in Jesus, a rest compatible with the most multiform service, the most unceasing activity; that can neither be communicated to the soul by rest of body (though it may be typified by it) nor destroyed by its activities, a rest of the body could no more attain the souls rest in Jesus than the blood of bulls and goats, the cleansing of the conscience to both it is still necessary for Jesus to come for he only is the body of the sabbath and the end of the sacrifices.

The sabbatical year also had a clear reference to the rest of the land a very far off, the heavenly Canaan and beautifully shadowed forth the manner of the supply of the wants of that land, it came pouring forth in rich abundance from the royal hand that rules there, for it is Emanuel's land without the labour of those who live amidst its abounding wonders, therefore neither man nor ox, nor ass, was to labour but to eat at the Lord's table continually. The sabbatical year shewed therefore the manner of the rest of all creation, but the sons and daughters of the Most High whilst they partook of this with all creation had yet a deeper rest shadowed forth by the sabbatical day. This was as I have before shewn the sign of the souls rest in Jesus. But Christ is the body of both and all the ordinances. He is the bread of Heaven and the rest of the soul in heaven and on earth, by which those live who have found him indeed the Prince of Peace. And if these are not the senses in which Christ is the body, I should feel greatly obliged by our author shewing in what respect he is the body and Lord of the Sabbath.

But let us consider a little further the commands relative to the holy observance of the sabbath, its provisions are then :—

1st. No fire shall be lit in all thy habitations.

2d. Thou shalt not do any work, neither thy son nor thy daughter.

3d. Thy man-servant nor maid-servant.

4th. Nor thy cattle, nor the stranger that is within thy gates.

If you then ask me, how men can pray to be inclined to keep this day holy, *specifying the manner of the holiness*, and yet light fires; employ servants in cooking food, and horses and men in carrying or driving them about, the answer supplied is this by the author, the strictness of observance (that is the liberty to violate every precept of God and set up others of our own) is also changed by the same authority, that instituted the day, then it is changed, if its strictness is mitigated it is changed; but this assertion appears to me without a shadow of truth in it, and at all events the proof lies with our author, and would be introducing Christ as breaking that very law he came to fulfil, the healing the sick is not forbidden, this Christ did, but light a fire, labour himself, servant or cattle he never did so far as scripture reveals, all he broke down was the superstitious additions of the Pharisees, till all was fulfilled, not one jot or tittle of the law was neglected by Jesus, he fulfilled it to the very letter.

THE LORD'S DAY.

The Lord's day of the New Testament for worship breaking bread as an Apostolic institution, I fully admit, delight in and observe; but all pharisacial rules about its observance I reject as our Lord rejected the pharisacial substitutions of their own, to what God had written in his word, and as I have before observed, I should feel the enjoining bodily rest on the Gentile Church, as a part of that service as great a sin as enjoining circumcision or sacrifices. But on this point I would observe, that since the minds of many are as much bound by traditional additions to this blessed day, as the Jews were to those additions to the Lord's sabbath. It becomes necessary to pursue a very similar course to that which our Lord pursued, with the bigotted Jews, to whom he gave place by subjection? no not for a moment, but on the contrary *He* took every opportunity to trample under foot these additions of men, doubtless there were many in his day who said to him what harm in allowing a little additional strictness in the observance of the sabbath, why run the risk of offending all the Jews, and weakening the power of your own ministry, by taking every opportunity to wound this the People's most cherished notion? It was doubtless because he saw that in the mass all this pretended zeal for their mode of observance, sprung from pure hypocrisy, shewn by their utter disregard to others that really were God's, and written as it were with a sunbeam, and also for the benefit of others who were sincere, our Lord seemed to desire to lay down this principle, the importance of adhering *to what is written*; if you once allow men to set up a divine claim to obedience, in one thing which is merely human, you open the floodgates to making the law of God or Christ of none effect, by mens traditions I may perhaps here just observe, that I asserted the name Sabbath, was never given to the Lord's day, till more than two centuries after Christ. Our author brings in the FOURTH CENTURY a doubtful quotation, from a doubtful author, who says, that our Lord changed the day from the sabbath to the first day of the week, this I take for granted proves our author had no better (even human) authority. In further explaining the historical bearing of this question I shall quote from a reply I have written to another attack, by one not content with the decalogue, but who roams at large taking, what he approves, bending the old to the new, or the new to the old, as it suits his judgment of how things ought to be. " The pious and learned Neander, unhesitatingly states the end of the second century, as the time when cessation from ordinary occupations began on the Lord's day

THE LORD'S DAY.

in the Church. The commission that sat in 1540, on the state of religion in the Church of England, decided that the keeping of every seventh day was only a ceremonial institution, and the language of Tindal the translator of the English Bible is most decided to the same point. Justin Martyr also says, that the Christians for the very purpose of drawing the line of separation more clear, between themselves and the Jews in this particular, always went about their ordinary occupations after worship was over, which was generally before mid-day ; and if they lived in the midst of Jewish converts to avoid giving them offence, they worshipped with them on their Sabbath, shewing that the transfer of the day and its character on the death of Christ in the Church from the 7th day to the 1st, is a mere fiction, and in Justin's controversy with Trypho the Jew. The Jew confesses the commandments of *the Gospel to be great and admirable, so much so, that there is reason to fear none will observe them.* But what is most offensive to the Jew is that the Christians according to this their Law differ in nothing from Heathens, neither through feasts, nor the Sabbath, nor circumcision, and still it is written, that every soul is to be destroyed that is not circumcised the 8th day. Now to these objections Justin answers, that the Mosaic law cannot be of absolute necessity because Moses was the first who gave it, and many attained salvation before him. Again, as to circumcision, he says if this had been necessary, God would not have formed Abraham or Adam in uncircumcision, and as to the Sabbath he says, nor would scripture have mentioned so many who were saved without a Sabbath, just the same as Abraham was counted just before his circumcision. Was not God the same God in Enoch's time, as in the patriarchs afterwards? If thou who wert under the law wert saved the same as Noah, and the patriarchs, it is only because there are in the law so many things belonging to the whole divine will. Here then the christian of the 2d century defends himself against the attack of the Jew, not by saying, we differ from the heathen by a Sabbath any more than by circumcision, but simply by declaring, they were not parts of the whole divine will. How would our modern Sabbatarians have argued this point? my object is to prove Justin had no notion of the Sabbath as existing in his time. And though in Tertullians time Jewish Analogies burst in on the Church, on all sides, an allusion to any connection between the Lord's day and the Sabbath of the Jews, is never once instituted by any writer, and when Constantine began to legislate for the Church in the 3d Century concerning the observance of the Lord's day as a festival, though he requires all magistrates and public officers in *Cities* to suspend their duties, yet he expressly excludes from the operations of this law, *the open country and works of agriculture, sowing corn, and binding up the vines.* Yet even down as low as Theodosius in the Council of " Orleans in 338, when he prohibited even works in the fields, it was not with the slightest reference to Moses or the Decalogue, but simply that the people may make more haste to Church, yet even this council notwithstanding its object was still farther to circumscribe the freedom of the Lord's day with respect to ordinary occupations on grounds of expediency adds that *to hold it unlawful to travel with horses, cattle and carriages, to prepare food, &c. savours more of Judaism than Christianity.*"

Ignatius has also these remarkable words. Be not deceived with strange doctrines, nor with old fables which are unprofitable, for if we still continue to live according to the Jewish law, we do confess ourselves not to have received grace. For even the most holy prophets lived according to Christ Jesus, and for this cause were they persecuted, being inspired by his grace, to convince the unbelievers and disobedient that there is one God, who has manifested himself by Jesus Christ his Son, who is his eternal word, who in all things pleased Him that sent him. Wherefore if they who were brought up in these ancient laws, came nevertheless to the newness of hope, no longer observing Sabbaths, but keeping the Lord's day (36) in which also our life is sprung up by him and through his death, whom yet some deny ; by which mystery we have been brought to believe and therefore wait that we may be formed the disciples of Jesus Christ, *our only Master*, how shall we be able to live different from him, whose disciples the very prophets themselves being, did by the Spirit expect him as their Master. And therefore he whom they justly waited for being come, raised them up from the dead. Let us not then

(36) How clear the distinction between these two days in the mind of Justin. The Sabbath was rest, irrespective of worship, the Lord's day worship, irrespective of rest, the Lord's ordinance was broken in the Sabbath by not resting, on the Lord's day by not worshipping.

be insensible of his goodness; for should he have dealt with us according to our works, we had not now had a being, wherefore being become his disciples, let us learn to live according to the *rules of Christianity* : (37) for whosoever is called by any other name besides this, he is not of God. Lay aside therefore, the old and sour and evil leaven, and be ye changed into the new leaven, which is Jesus Christ. Be ye salted in him, lest any one among you should be corrupted; for by your Saviour ye shall be judged. It is absurd to name Jesus Christ, and to Judaize. For the Christian religion did not embrace the Jewish, but the Jewish the Christian; that so every tongue that believed might be gathered unto God."

Indeed to Sabbatise and Apostatise were nearly equally opposed in primitive times. The sin of Sabbath breaking is never brought forward, the sin of Sabbath keeping continually, and it must never be forgotten, that this was not by men who opposed the Sabbath as part of the *Jewish law* but who allowed it to the Jewish prejudices and would rather than *offend them keep it with them*, yet never would allow its character to be put on the Lord's day and for this purpose they would not kneel or fast ever on the Lord's day. Now if the 4th commandment was felt binding on the Gentiles, would not the Sabbatizers have brought this forward with irresistable weight against their opponents, to justify their Jewish tendencies, but it never is

(37) Justin's rule of life seems pretty clear from this, not to have been the Decalogue.

by any writer for more than three centuries. I say three merely to avoid dispute, but to this day it is equally unknown to the Greek, Armenian, Chaldean or any of the eastern Churches with which I have had intercourse.

"I do not refer to these things" as authority with myself, but for others my sole ground is, that in the whole New Testament, not one command to observe it, or one threat against those who do not observe it as a day *of rest and freedom from ordinary occupation*, as many now insist on is to be found. And neither does Saint Barnabus the most Jewish of the Apostolic fathers, in the list, in which he details most minutely what a Christian man ought to do, name the keeping either of a Sabbath or any sacred day; nor in his list of the sins of those who quit the good way in which a Christian man ought to walk, does he name the violation of any such day. Yet after this, if any wish to keep it really as a Jewish Sabbath, without one precept from the New Testament, for it, and the History of the whole Christian Church against it, for more than two centuries, let them; kindling no fire in their habitations, nor allowing their cattle or their servants to do any manner of work, and whosoever doeth let him be put to death; not with the mockery they now throw on it, breaking every precept about the Sabbath, they pray to God to incline their hearts to keep. I shall then respect their motives and my only prayer is that they may keep it to the Lord, but not set themselves up to Judge others who do not see with their eyes, unless they have scripture to adduce, which

I have never yet discovered. For myself I delight in the Lord's day and its holy blessed occupations as one of my Lord's most graciously allowed ways of devoting all my time to Him. I keep it because I love it, it is so delightful to have especial seasons continually recurring to remember in breaking the bread and drinking the Cup, the broken body of Jesus the pledge of the Churches unity as one bread until he come again whom our eyes long to see. But does not your heart rejoice in keeping Good Friday, yet I am not in bondage to it, but I love all times and seasons that remind me of his voluntary humiliation in order to his ultimate glory, I will join any saints on any days if their object be to bring glory to Jesus, or remember his matchless ways, but never as a form or mere ordinance of man, for Christ has blotted out the hand writing of ordinances, nailing it to his cross in order that we might not be judged any more about meat or drink, or holy days, or the new moons or the sabbath, which were but shadows of which Christ was the body, Col. ii. 14, 17."

As to the seventh day being consecrated in Paradise we have no record of it but in Gen. ii. where no notion of *bodily rest as such* is enjoined that the seventh day has ever been distinguished in some sort from the rest, I think is most probable as a day of public worship and sacrafice among God's children and regarded much as our Lord's day was among the primative Christians only varying in the manner of its observances under different dispensations according to the light the Spirit threw on what would be acceptable service to God. But that this day was ever kept in such sort as among the Jews after the institution in the wilderness, there is no evidence for it but much against it in the first place the word Sabbath never occurs till Exodus, though the seventh day does frequently and when Nehemiah ix. 13, 14, refers to this institution he makes the wilderness the place where it originated. Thou camest down also upon Mount Sanai, and spakest with them from heaven, and gavest them right judgments, and true laws, good statutes and commandments. And madest known unto them thy holy Sabbath, and commandest them precepts, statutes, and laws, by the hand of Moses thy Servant: also Ezkl. xx. 10, 12. Wherefore I caused them to go forth out of the land of Egypt and brought them *into the wilderness*. Moreover, also, I gave them my Sabbaths, to be a sign between me and them, that they might know that I am the Lord that sanctify them. Philo the Jew seemed to think that they had forgotten during their Egyptian Captivity their Sabbaths, and that this was only a re-institution but as Dr. Jennings in his Jewish antiquities, says (if the Israelites had forgot the original Sabbath, God certainly had not; and it is very improbable he would have *commanded them to travel from* Elim to Sin on the day, he had consecrated to sacred rest which he did on the preceding day that in course should have been the Sabbath, namely the 15th of the month, the 1st Sabbath on record as being kept being on the 22nd. For the children of Israel never journeyed, but at the command of God, (See Appendix B) Exod. xiii. 21 Numb. ix. 18 and with reference to the passage in Gen. above alluded to, the author of a Dictionary of the Bible in three volumes, published in 1759, says. The greatest part of the fathers and commentators hold that the benediction and sanctification of the Sabbath mentioned by Moses in the beginning of Gen. signifies only that appointment then made of the seventh day, to be afterwards solemnized and sanctified by the Jews. It does not appear from any passage of Scripture, that the ancient patriarchs have observed the Sabbath, or that God had any design to oblige them thereto—Ezek. (xx. 12, 20) says expressly that the Sabbath and the other feasts of the Jews; are signs that God has given to his people to distinguish them from other nations, I gave them my " Sabbaths, to be a sign between me and them " that they might know that I am the Lord that " sanctify them" and again," hallow my Sabbaths and " they shall be a sign between me and you that he may " know that I am the Lord your God" and Moses in Deut. v. 15 the Lord hath brought thee out of Egypt, therefore the Lord thy God command thee to keep the Sabbath day! Justin Martyr, Tertullian, Eusebius, and St. Bernard, advance as a matter not to be doubted that neither the patriarchs before the deluge, nor those which came afterwards observed the Sabbath. All the above reasonings only are of value (the question being one where the Scriptures are silent) as setting the opinions of the ancients against the opinions of the moderns.

In fact it would be difficult to conceive how that institution could be regarded as a sign between God and the children of Israel if it was common to all nations, and the very use of the word, remember, implies that it was a thing likely to be forgotten through inadvertance, and newness &c. and is not what naturally would be used or referring to what never could have been forgotten, had it been the universal practice of all preceding generations. In fact the children of Israel going out to gather manna, (See Appendix C) and the man to gather sticks, and Moses' ignorance how to treat the case judically, stamps newness on the character of the institution.

I will now take up in conclusion the second point, namely the importance of the enquiry.

1st.—In relation to truth.

2d.—In reference to the glory of Jesus and his exaltation.

TRUTH.

1st. As to truth there is a unity in it with itself and no man can interfere with this, without endangering the beauty and stability of the whole. A false view leads us to judge one another and doubt one another, and obstruct each others service to our common Lord where we ought not and being under the appearance of holy zeal about God's things leads us to follow Saul of Tarsus often, but too closely. What was the effect on the minds of the Pharisees having adopted erroneous views about the Sabbath, and having appended as they thought stricter notions to it, why that it extinguished in their eyes all the glory of the Son of God and made them seek in satan's power, the explanation of all the purest acts of his devotion to their interests, and they did all they could by accusing him of breaking the law and the Sabbath, to obstruct his ministry and his teaching, and is not the appending stricter and other notions to the Lord's day than you can say " it is written" to, the same. I desire also to feel myself subject to every word of God in the sense and meaning that I believe God has given to it. And what more does the author's instruction embrace about the due observance of the Lord's day than what I fully allow? he says, we ought to meet together for breaking of bread, and distributing to the poor, these two objects I have ever felt the proper objects which characterise the Lords day, these are all the texts he has given for the due observance of the Lord's day, and therefore I presume all he could find, these I have ever kept if possible and done my best to induce others to keep. However, this will not satisfy. I must call it a Sabbath and feel myself under the law of the Jewish Sabbath, and if I will only allow this, then I may take a dispensation in common with our author to break every precept contained in the whole books of Moses as a direction how to observe it; man may acquit me of responsibility, but my heart feels I could not on such a principle hold up my face before a heathen, how much less before God, our author says the law of the sabbath was originally written on the heart of man, (38) and suppose I take his principle as true and use the decalogue definition about the holyness of the Sabbath as stated above to a heathen, if he were to retort on me and tell me I break every precept of it. If I were to tell him as our author does his readers that the code of Christ has changed it, I should be asserting what I believe has not the shadow of truth,

(38) How then can it be a shadow of which Christ is the body I leave our author to explain Col. iii.—

and that which would make him feel such a law, was worse than no law, meaning a variety of things it did not say, and nothing that it did. And for which after all, I could bring no action of the Lord to warrant, nor any Precept in all the New Testament to prove. And surely if a heathen could see me interpreting thus away the words of God that I professed to follow or to believe, because it suited my convenience it would be doubtless teaching him to practice the same Spirit of explaining away the plainest precepts to suit his; at all events I could not so act without feeling myself degraded in my own eyes, and that of every heathen I used such an argument with.

Besides *truth* obliges me to teach that the ministration on stones is done away, is abolished, had no glory in comparison with that which remains that they cannot be heirs together, that it is disannulled from its weakness, that all these things were but rudiments in the hand of the school master until Christ, who brought in LOVE the perfect law of liberty. What I owe therefore to *truth*, obliges me to state what God has written regardless of all consequences. I see my Lord did it in perfectly similar circumstances and all those who have ever stood against any error of doctrine in favor of which the passions and interests of men have been engaged, have suffered for it and must.

Hitherto I have directed my observations to meet and remove particular objections, I purpose now to conclude my remarks on our author's work by shewing that by making Moses the lawgiver of the Christain Church, and the Decalogue the rule of life for Christ's

Bride, our author directly opposes the design of God the Father.

EXALTATION OF JESUS THE DESIGN OF GOD.

Secondly, in reference to the glory of Christ and his exaltation. This design of God the Father is thus expressly shewn in Colossians, where speaking of the Father, Paul says, that he hath delivered us from the power of darkness, and translated us into the kingdom of his dear Son, in whom we have redemption through his blood, even the forgiveness of sins, who is the image of the invisible God, the first born of every creature, for by him were all things created that are in heaven, and that are in earth, visible and invisible, whether they be thrones, or dominions, or principalities, or powers, all things were created *by* him, and *for* him, and he is before all things, and by him all things consist and he is head of the body the Church, who is the beginning, the first born from the dead, *that in all things he might have the pre-eminence.* God's purpose I think cannot be more plainly stated than hereby the Apostle of the uncircumcision and surely if the Gentiles wish to know their duties, relative to their Head, it is for them here to contemplate their heavenly Father's design, and then ask themselves whether by making Moses the Lawgiver and God's own Son the commentator, they are really giving the Son of God that preeminence, which the Father seeks for him, namely, equal honor with himself. Let us now for a moment dwell on one or two of those offices which Christ fills in connection with his church in relation to this subject.

CHRIST AS A JUDGE.

In considering Christ in the character of a Judge, the first question that arises in the mind is what is the nature of those laws which he will then, administer, for surely, now, no question can more deeply concern every child of Adam, than rightly understanding while the day of salvation is ours, the nature and principles that govern the judgments of that day, when all shall stand before the judgment seat of Christ, to receive according to the deeds done in the body; in things of the earth mistakes may be rectified, but an error here will find the soul who has committed it where Dives was, sensible too late that his standard of holiness had been a phantom of his own. In the passage I have above quoted from the Colossians, the Holy Ghost states that Christ was the creator of all things, the image of the invisible God and made head over all things to the Church, which is elsewhere called his bride (Rev. 21-9 to 3-29.) that in all things he might have the pre-eminence, Heb. ii. 1-3. If we look again at Heb. x. 26-29. We see the law of Christ and sinning against it is plainly shewn to be both a different and much more deadly thing, than sinning against the law of Moses. With which it is CONTRASTED, and when again we see the Lord represented, 2 Thess : 1. 8, coming in flames of fire with his mighty angels to take vengeance on those who know not God, it is also declared those shall meet the same fate, not who make not the Decalogue or whole Sinai covenant their rule of life, but those who OBEY not the GOSPEL of our Lord Jesus Christ.

surely then we see it was not God's design that we should set up Moses' Law as the rule to detect sin by. Again the parable in the 25th of Matthew, which shews the principles of Christ's judgment at his appearing and kingdom, you see not the condemned charged either with the breach of the decalogue as a whole or any precept in it, but simply for having lived regardless of Christ and not given themselves to positive service, it was not for what they HAD done they were condemned, but what they had NOT done, and that not to Moses, but to Jesus, but if the instrument to convict the soul of sin by under Christ's rule and government be the decalogue, how is it that the Lord Jesus, the Judge of Quick and Dead, never makes any allusion to it, is it not because as he said " my words shall Judge you in the last day." Again, how many times does the Father draw our attention to the Son, by this or a similar expression. "This is my beloved Son hear ye Him," and when our Lord in parables shews forth his Father's conduct, he represents after all other means had failed in sending servant after servant, he *at last* sent his only Son, evidently intending to shew his pre-eminence. But let us examine a little more attentively those parables that were designed to exhibit the character of the last Judgment, for some may still think, though Christ will sit on the throne as Judge, yet the decalogue will be his instrument of condemnation. Let us then again refer to the parables and try this by facts; our blessed Lord has given us various illustrations as I have observed, in those parables which relate to the Judgment, that is to take place at the end of this dispensation. In several cases our Lord represents himself as sitting as a King to judge his subjects, and in not one is the violation of the decalogue alluded to or any precept in it, as the grounds of condemnation to a single sinner. The 1st Matt. xviii. 23, 25, is the condemnation of the wicked servant who having been pardoned much, takes his fellow by the throat saying pay me that thou owest; Matt. xx ii. 1, 11. Here we have the three causes of condemnation, the first, the contempt of the Gospel, the second, against those open enemies who not only reject it altogether, but destroy its messengers, and thirdly, those who receive it but feignedly, not having on a wedding garment; xxv, 1, 13 of Matt. the foolish Virgins for having no oil in their vessels and want of preparation and watchfulness for the return of the Son of Man again; Matt. xxi, 14, 30. The condemnation here is for having a talent and wrapping it in a napkin; again, xxv, 31, 46 we have condemnation upon those who having ability yet saw Christ's members, hungry, and thirsty, naked, sick and in prison and ministered not unto them. Again Luke xvii, 15, 31. The condemnation of Dives is that he was clothed in purple and fared sumptuously every day, and selfishly neglected Lazarus at his gate. Again Luke xix. 11. we have not only here the same as in Matthew the punishment of a slothful servant wrapping up the Lord's treasure, but we have also this declaration of the determination of the Lord Jesus concerning those who will not have him to reign over them. Now in all these parables, there is not one allusion to the decalogue as an instrument of conviction, not one of them is accused of the breach of either of the commandments, but all are judged on the ground of DISLOYALTY to Jesus, just as when Christ convinced Paul of Tarsus of sin, it was not by the decalogue, but by saying, *why persecutest thou me?* for Christ has shewn that it is not only disloyalty to him, to say, we will not have this man to reign over us, but to withhold the proofs of love from those who are bone of his bone, and flesh, of his flesh or to inflict evil upon them. All the condemnation in the Lord's judgment is against the absence of loyalty and love to himself as King in Zion, and his members, because men disregarded that which Christ commanded, his disciples to preach; go says he, and preach the Gospel to every creature, he that believeth and is baptised shall be saved, and he that believeth not shall be damned, and therefore Christ condemns the world of sin, not for its breach of the decalogue, but as he himself declares the SPIRIT shall convince the world of sin, of righteousness and judgment " of sin because they *believe not on me*" this is the sin that includes every other as belief in Jesus, is the grace that *includes* every other. If now any one should be still led to ask, is not this undervaluing the law? I would answer no, it was holy, just and good, and perfect *for the ends* the Father designed when publishing it, to the Jews it was added because of transgression TILL the seed should come, and abolished, when he came because of weakness and imperfection in attaining the *ultimate* ends of God's mercy to man. I assert however that the law of the Spirit of life in Christ Jesus, which sets us free from the law of sin and death is holier, and better, and that the Lord Jesus the Creator and Lord of Moses his Wonderful Counsellor, who was the stream that followed him in the wilderness, is entitled to more honor than Moses in every respect and that this was the Father's design in making every knee bow to him.

CHRIST AS KING.

Secondly. Scripture contemplates Jesus as King; now if you separate legislation from the kingly office what do you leave it, if you make the king the commentator, on the laws of his servant rather than the originator of his own, do you not destroy his headship and give him a servants place, when God has given him a Son's, who has exalted him above every name that is named of things in heaven and things on the earth and things under the earth, but above all, Head over all things to the Church. Would it not appear strange if HE by whom and for whom all things were created and to whom of the Father is committed all judgment, for the very purpose, that all men should honor the Son even as the Father, if he had to direct his Prisoners at the Bar to Moses as the Lawgiver and himself only as the expounder. The apostle Paul styles our Lord, " God over all, blessed for evermore," now if it really be God's design that this honor should be paid the only begotten one, and as our blessed Lord himself says, if they do not honor him neither do they the Father, it is no ordinary boldness to take the step of doing such open violence to Christ's honor, as to put his bride the Church under Moses for her rule of life, and what does she hear when she does go to Moses for a rule of life? any words like her own Lord's? if ye love me, keep my commandments; I go away and prepare a place for you and if I go and prepare a place for you, I will come again and take you to myself" no but do not commit idolatry, do not commit adultery, do not steal, do not bear false witness, but is this the kind of language that love uses to win the holy worship, chastity and truth of a faithful bride, is it not putting her on a footing with those murderers of fathers and murderers of mothers, whoremongers, &c. for whom Paul says the law was written, not the righteous for whom he declares it was not written, is this what the free born bride of Christ might expect from her departing Lord, to keep her footsteps right? or does it not savour more of the language of slavery and bondage of the son of the bond woman, which is mount Sinai in Arabia, than the son of the free of Jerusalem which is above.

CHRIST AS A LAWGIVER.

Thirdly. Let us now consider Christ as truly and properly a Lawgiver in the 60th and 108th Psalms. Judah is called God's Lawgiver; now this cannot refer to Moses who was of the tribe of Levi, whereas our Lord was of the tribe of Judah. Again, Isaiah says chap. xxxiii. 17, 22. " Thine eyes shalt see the king in his beauty, they shall behold the land that is very far off, for the Lord is our Judge, the Lord is our Lawgiver the Lord is our King he will save us. And this passage Calvin himself, to whose opinion our author seems to give so great a weight, allows has its consummation in Christ. Here then I think we have again a clear declaration, that that Jesus who was their King and Judge (for all judgment is committed unto him) is also called the Lawgiver, the Lawgiver of the tribe of Judah. But Paul also declares that when the Priesthood was changed, there was of necessity also a *change in the law*, if Christ were not a Lawgiver by whom was this change to be made, for I think few would deny that as high, if not higher Legislative authority is required to change, than to enact a law, as it implies supersession of what went before. But Moses himself said, a Prophet shall the Lord your God raise up unto you like unto me, *him shall ye hear* and the soul that shall not hear, that prophet shall be cut of from among the people. Now if Christ were not a *legislating* Prophet, how could he be like Moses, for this was his peculiar distinguishing characteristic and in this he was only the type, creature and servant of that great *Lawgiver*, who was to come to reign over the Gentiles and in whom they were to trust and for whose " LAW the *Gentiles were to wait*" yes Christ is that one Lawgiver, who is able, as James says, both to kill and to destroy, and not Moses. (39.)

But before concluding this subject I would add one remark more on the following quotation of our author's from Calvin on Matt. 5 "away then with that error that the defects of the law are here corrected by Christ, for Christ is not to be supposed a *New Lawgiver* who has added something to the *eternal righteousness of his Father*, but he is to be heard as a faithful interpreter that we may know the real character and tendency of the law and how far it extends." Now to these observations I would only say, whether Christ be a new Lawgiver or not, he is the giver of a new Law or rule of life to believers,

---

(39) Our author in the 80th page of his work, when commenting on the meaning of the word Lawgiver in James not only denies that it refers to Christ, but declares, James never mentions Chris'ts name in all his Epistle as Christ " whereas in the first verse of the first chapter he calls himself the servant of God and the *Lord Jesus Christ* in the first verse of 2d chapter, he says, my brethren have not the faith of *our Lord Jesus Christ*. The Lord of Glory—with respect of persons." Here then are two distinct appeals to Christ—as Lord, beside the 7 verse of 5th chapter where he says " Be patient unto the coming *of the Lord*.—Our author also asserts that there is no Lawgiver but God the Father, at all events Moses is called the Lawgiver, Numbers xxi. 18, and when we read James we must never forget he was writing to Jewish Christians, to whom circumcision, sacrifices, Sabbaths and all parts of the law were in use and not Gentiles. See Pole Syn. Crit: also in loco where he says " Legislator nobis non Moses sed Christus" to us Moses is not the Lawgiver but Christ, he also states that the Latin Syriac and Arabic versions add to the word Lawgiver $\kappa\alpha\iota$ $\kappa\rho\iota\tau\eta$ and Judge which plainly shews to whom they considered the term Lawgiver to apply.

for I do not deny that it was Christ who wrote with his finger the ministration of death written and graven on stones FIFTY DAYS AFTER the sacrifice of the typical paschal Lamb, when the sword of the avenging angel, which swept away the first born of Egypt, entered not the dwellings of the children of Israel, but I contend these were but types and shadows of his own free sacrifice of himself as the very paschal Lamb of God, and his sending down FIFTY DAYS AFTER his new Law from the Mount of the throne of God, and writing it on the fleshly tables of his disciples hearts by the Spirit. As to adding to his Father's eternal righteousness; surely that Law of which God says it made nothing perfect, could not be the full display of the Father's eternal righteousness. The fact is, there is great confusion here apparently in some minds, no one can more fully admit than I do that in God the Father's mind, there is a fixed and immutable rule or standard of moral order and beauty, that is like all his attributes infinite and unchangeable. But I deny on the authority of God's own word that the legislation of the Jews whether in the decalogue or elsewhere was a full transcript of this, immutable rule. A legislator has respect not only to the perfection of his own nature and conceptions, but the capability to bear in his subjects, and therefore when his disciples pleaded Moses allowance of that which Christ stigmatizes by the name of adultery, he tells them, it was only allowed for the hardness of their hearts, a statute that was not good, this explanation of our Lord proves to me to a demonstration, that the law had reference in its whole character to the state of the people, for whom the laws were enacted and I consider our Lord's declaration, that he had many things to say to his disciples, but that they could not then bear them, an instance of a similar principle being recognized; as well as when Paul complains of his converts, as being unable to bear what otherwise he would have taught them, being such as needed milk like babes, not strong meat like men: again concerning Melchizedeck, Paul declares he had many things to say, but they were dull of hearing and could not bear them. Relative to the author's challenge to shew him one statute (40) that was not good, I not only repeat God's own declaration in the passage in Ezekiel, and " I gave them statutes that were not good, and laws by which a man should not live" but I give this exposition of our Lord that that which the more perfect mind of God sees it now fit under the Gentile and more perfect dispensation to stigmatize as adultery was allowed them, though not good for the hardness of their heart; our author very conveniently leaves out "therefore *I (God)* GAVE *them* statutes that were not good." There are many passages in scripture where God is said to give them UP to evil where it implies a leaving them alone; but I am not aware of one where God says I gave them when he did not give actively, if I did I could accept his interpreta-

(40) Does our author not admit that he does not love those statutes concerning slavery, divorce, &c. and is not this conceding, that he does not think them good.

tion of Ezekiel as possible, but still Christ's declaration admitting the general principle remains untouched as well as the Holy Ghost's by Paul, that the law made *nothing perfect,* for when God says I gave them statutes that were not good, I do not understand him to mean statutes opposed to essential morality, but simply less perfect than his love would have desired and his holiness chosen for them, such as those connected with polygamy, concubinage, slavery, and which were as much God's statutes as the decalogue, and this his holy design he finally manifested by his only begotten Son. If I were asked how I could account for Calvin expressing so strong an opinion, I should say in the same way as I account for his companion and friend Beza's mistranslation before pointed out of the 5th of Matt. in opposition to the universal usage of the language, and in direct opposition also to all his predecessors; it owes I believe its origin to what Dr. Campbell calls, being too much of a polemic to be in all cases, the one a faithful translator, the other a faithful commentator. Their hatred as well as that of all the reformers to popery led them too much to think the extreme opposite of what the Papist did was right, and seeing that the Papists turned the Lord's day into a day of worldly pleasure and dissipation. They thought they would be doing God service, apparently by throwing a judaical strictness into it, by setting up the decalogue description of it as still binding, in opposition to the New Testament and all Christian antiquity from which it may be observed, the learned Calvin brings no proof to justify its revival, were as his wise path would have been to have shewn that its true object was retirement for public worship and religious service and that they had better not rest from secular avocations at all, than to rest from these to pursue pleasures, riots, and amusements, that would have been disgraceful to a Christian on any day, and in doing this he would have had abundant support from all early antiquity, for they would have disallowed on any day, those things which the Papists chose the Lord's day for carrying on. These feelings about the Lord's day were participated in by Knox and the Scotch reformers and by the Puritans and their transatlantic brethren so that it became to them and their descendants from education and habit very much what the Sabbath was to the Scribes and Pharisees of our Lord's time a view so rooted in their affections so devotedly the object of their veneration, that to touch, but the border of their apparently holy prejudice, involved participating with our Lord in a rejection as far as their voice could effect it of the bold innovator from the bosom of the family of God and what is so strange is that those very persons who would condemn the Jews for judging the Lord by their traditions and not the word, are themselves involved in the very same guilt, so easy is it to build the tombs of the dead prophets in order to soothe and quiet the conscience when meditating the destruction of the living members of the redeemed family.

DEFENCE OF MY FRIENDS.

I have ever endeavoured to avoid all personal allusions when discussing subjects connected with truth though it is often difficult when personally attacked, because I am persuaded it must stand on a far more stable base, than that of personal consistency or inconsistency to be of any real value to the Church of God, but since the Pamphlet united my friends with me in its charges I must be excused saying a few words in their vindication as to these charges.

ANTINOMIANISM.

1st. As to the Antinomianism or lawlessness charged on us; the time was when it would have been more difficult than now to meet it by a direct practical refutation, for it was but a few years since, when there were but few indeed in England, who were united in judgment, as to many of those points here so strongly objected against; they have now increased to near 200 assemblies, more or less numerous in England and Ireland of all ranks, now, surely had preaching Christ's life simply as our example, and His and the Apostles precepts as their rule of life, and citizenship in heavenly places with Christ Jesus even now, and the constant exhortations if risen with Christ, to set our hearts not on the earth but on those things that are with him at God's right hand, tended to lawlessness toward God ; it would have long ere this have manifested itself, but who that knows them, would be prepared to say those connected with the establishment are more exemplary in every moral duty that belongs to an exalted christian walk, than those here designated as my friends. Do they devote to the Lord's service, more of their time, more of their means, more of their unpaid service? (except it be the remuneration of obloquy and reproach) does the author really believe the members of the establishment carry farther or deeper than those he has so disparagingly treated the principles of the renunciation of the world and the consecration of themselves, as reasonable living sacrifices unto God, by the non-conformity of their lives, to the course of this present evil world, and by that transformation which arises from the renewing of the mind by the Spirit's power? I do not believe any one would say so, who intimately knew them, nor that those assemblies I have alluded to as spiritual societies, would lose by the closest comparison between them and the most favored of the assemblies of the establishment, I believe as a whole they earnestly desire to trample under foot, all lawlessness *natural* and *spiritual*, casting down reasonings and every high thing that exalteth itself against the knowledge of God, and bringing into captivity every thought to the obedience of Christ. My fear is that it may not continue and increase, but whilst I feel it right to say thus much for those who are here alluded to as my friends, I wish clearly to be understood as not making them responsible for my opinions in every particular, nor myself for theirs—we have by the separate study of God's word alone, arrived at a number of similar, if not the same results, yet on some points perhaps they would not concur with me, and in others I might not be able to concur with them, indeed I should look upon it as the certain mark of a sectarian spirit, growing up, that you could judge from one of the opinions of all, in all particulars on which opinions, and often very decided ones are formed by some; it would shew the absence of individuality of thought and realization; for whilst I believe that an individual study of the scriptures will produce a marvellous unity in all, the grand essentials of truth, it will be attended with as great a diversity in many things about which men are now often so dogmatical, and the reason of this diversity is, that the spirit has not revealed fully his mind concerning them.

ON QUITTING THE ESTABLISHMENT.

2d. Our author refers to my leaving the establishment as that which was forsaking the fountain of my blessings. That dawning of truth which made the common aims of human life a blank to me, I gratefully acknowledge I owe to one instrumentally who wore the badge of the establishment, yet it was to one who knew far too well where the strength of the Gospel's transforming power lay, to press on the conscience those precepts which every fel on in Newgate knows and disregards, no he taught me to feel the love against which I was sinning, the *grace* I was trampling under foot, and if I have ever been constrained at all to live unto him, who died for me, it is by the power of that love which constrained Paul, he knew the Law worked wrath, not love, and above all this, that the only commission he held from Christ or his Spirit was to preach the gospel the glad tidings to every creature under heaven. But since the chord is touched, connected with the English establishment, which even now vibrates within me by bringing to my recollection scenes of trial and temporal loss in every way that could try the heart, that had ceased to care for itself, by the deep sorrow it occasioned others; I would state I had every inducement and desire to remain as I had ever been her faithful servant, with undivided heart I consecrated to her use, all I was and got except a simple provision for my family, and I allowed none to share it with her, and had my conscience been so constructed that I could have signed my unfeigned assent and consent to what I did not believe the truth of God, either to gratify my longing desire to remain within her pale, or for a piece of silver and a morsel of bread, or what was infinitely more powerful than all these, to meet the anxious wishes of those to whom I owed more than I could name, I should have escaped becoming the offscouring of all things, as I feel, I now am to so many whose good opinion I would gladly have preserved at any price less, than a guilty conscience; and I might have been moreover in the very same field of labour I now am in very different circumstances, but this I could not do, I first felt in my own conscience, convinced that many of the articles, canons and constitutions of the English Establishment, were opposed to the mind of God, in such particulars as vitiated her whole character, by constituting rules for admitting to and rejecting from ministry, in direct opposition to those of God. Thus far my enquiries had conducted me before a doubt, ever entered my mind that the foundation of her assumed spiritual authority, as well as the whole fabric, raised upon it was based upon the sand, and that the whole system with which they were connected was so ordered as to lay God's laws prostrate at the feet of man's, this left me and all who thought with me no alternative, but to protest against these limitations and restrictions the offspring of a worldly spirit, by fulfilling our duties as we best could, irrespective of them both to our Lord and the Church of the first born, and earnestly contend for the faith once delivered to the saints before the enablings of the Spirit were over-ruled and set aside by the regulations and institutions of men. I am not prepared to expect that our author or his friends would allow I had just reason, but neither would the Romish establishment allow the Protestants had cause for avoiding her on account of her perversions of truth and she might equally have pleaded how many of those, nay all who thus opposed her had been nourished up in her maternal bosom, but they felt and acted on the principle, that loyalty to Jesus was a higher virtue than allegiance to any human system, and that nothing could justify them either in participating in delusions they felt to be sinful themselves, or suffering them without a protest on her, whom they wished to see walking in the light of all that truth they themselves had realized, by turning once more to those living fountains the *word of the living God* which had been so long sealed up. The Protest, the reformers made against the errors of the Romish establishment, the Protest the old Prophet made against Jeroboams establishment, the prototype of all human establishments as well as Elijah's against that of Jezebel and Ahab are examples to us, that we must not follow a multitude to do evil, but witness against them though alone by following out all the truth the Lord reveals, lest he should shut us up in double darkness. If any establishment had claims to be spared it was God's own at Jerusalem, yet how severely did our Lord and all the prophets—" hew" her and certainly no blessing is ever pronounced on those who heal her slightly, or say peace, peace, when there is no peace.

Appendix A.

It is impossible to deny the merit of novelty to some of the reasonings of Archdeacon Stopford, in a work he has lately published, for he endeavours to persuade us that *rest* was only a secondary consideration in the observance of the Sabbath and *worship* the primary. Let us refer to Scripture. In Exodus xxxi. 13, 17. is to be found the following passage.

"Speak thou also unto the Children of Israel, saying, verily my Sabbaths ye shall keep, for it is a sign between me and you throughout your generations; that ye may know that I am the Lord who doth sanctify you. Ye shall keep the Sabbath therefore; for it is holy unto you: every one that defileth it, shall surely be put to death: for whosoever doeth any work therein, that soul shall be cut off from among his people. Six days may work be done; but in the Seventh is the Sabbath of rest, holy to the Lord: whosoever doeth any work on the Sabbath day, he shall surely be put to death. Wherefore the Children of Israel shall keep the sabbath, to observe the Sabbath throughout their generations, for a perpetual covenant. It is a sign between me and the Children of Israel for ever: for in six days the Lord made Heaven and Earth, and on the seventh day he rested, and was refreshed.

I confess this passage appears to me conclusive that rest was the primary idea in the Sabbath as its very name shews and this all the disputes between Our Lord and the Pharisees confirms, it was never about worship to God that the contest was but it was about how far natural humanity shewn in works of benevolence to men was to be considered more important than typical righteousness, or when one form of typical righteousness interfered with another as the labour of sacrifices with rest; which God had appointed to give place, and then rest of the Sabbath was to give place to the labour of the Sacrificial temple service, as the type of the pathway to all true rest in Jesus, was by shedding of blood, without which there could be no Sabbath to the Soul, and certainly the Apostle in the Hebrews looked on rest as the grand type, the antetype of which is to be realized by faith. Heb. iv. 1, 11.

Let us therefore fear, lest, a promise being left us of entering into his rest, any of you should seem to come short of it. For unto us was the Gospel preached, as well as unto them: but the word preached did not profit them, not being mixed with faith in them that heard it. For we which have believed do enter into rest, as he said, as I have sworn in my wrath, if they shall enter into my rest: although the works were finished from the foundation of the world. For he spake in a certain place of the seventh day on this wise, and God did rest the seventh day from all his works. And in this place again, if they shall enter into my rest. Seeing therefore it remaineth that some must enter therein, and they to whom it was first preached entered not in because of unbelief (again, he limiteth a certain day, saying in David, to day, after so long a time; as it is said, to day if ye will hear his voice, harden not your heart. For if Jesus had given them rest, then would he not afterward have spoken of another day. There remaineth therefore a rest to the people of God. For he that is entered into his rest, he also hath ceased from his own works, as God did from his.) Let us labour therefore to enter into that rest, lest any man fall after the same example of unbelief.

Our author seems to attach some peculiar notion to

Sanctification, but surely in Scripture this term is so used as to shew, that that is looked upon as sanctified which is done to God according to God's ordinance, separating it unto the uses for which God designed it, the sanctification of the Sabbath was to rest, the sanctified use of the vessels of the Sanctuary was to separate them unto the use to which God had appointed them, and thus the unbelieving wife is said to be sanctified by the husband, and the unbelieving husband sanctified by the wife, it seems therefore to me impossible *a priori* to determine, (previous to God's manifesting his will concerning it), what would be the sanctified use of any time, place, or thing, we may know all ought to be used to the Glory of God, but none but God can reveal what mode will bring glory to his Name.

Appendix B.

The following passage from Archdeacon Stopford's reply (page 57) to the Archbishop of Dublin's tract on the abrogation of the moral law having been brought to my notice as refuting the notion of the march of the Israelites the seventh day preceding that on which they kept their first Sabbath I think it right to introduce the whole passage from the work containing the opposing arguments and to point out the mistakes under which both the Archdeacon and his opponents in common appear to me to labour, from unacquaintance with the climate and circumstances of travelling in those countries in the midst of which these scenes are placed. The following is the passage from the Archdeacon's work.

"We are all agreed that the Israelites came to the wilderness of Sin on the 15th day of the second month, exactly a month after their departure from Epypt, but we agree no farther. The common error of these three great men* is the supposition, that quails were sent the evening of the fifteenth, and the manna next morning, and so on for six days, and that the Sabbath was on the twenty-second. All this I expect to shew to be erroneous by incontrovertible proof. And by the same kind of proof, I expect to establish the following to have been the real particulars and circumstances of the transaction. " I speak as unto wise men: Judge ye what I say." They came to the Wilderness of Sin in the evening of the fifteenth, the day of their journey from Elim. They continued murmering a great part of the night, in the course of which the quails and manna were promised through Moses, and at the same time he announced that the glory of the Lord, the symbol of the divine presence, should appear next morning, that is on the sixteenth, at which time it did appear, and then they were told by God himself that the quails should come in the following evening, and manna the next morning; that is, on the evening and morning of the seventeenth. That day on which these promises were given from the divine presence, was the sixteenth, and the seventh before the manna Sabbath (if I may so call it.) And on that day they did rest, because it was the Sabbath; a divine communication was granted, because it was the Sabbath, and the granting of the quails and manna was suspended until the day was over, (notwithstanding their urgent necessity,) because it was the sabbath. So soon as that day was over, viz at even, at six o'clock, which with them was the commencement of the next or first day of the week, or seventeenth of the month the quails came; and in the following morning of the same day, the manna was sent: and so on for six days, and the seventh was the manna Sabbath, which was the twenty-third day of the month and not the twenty second, as our authors suppose. If I establish these

* *Heylyn, Mede, and Bishop Bramhall.*

points, all their arguments fall flat to the ground, and the proof will be all in our favour. And I expect, moreover, to find in this Chapter, on close inspection, several intimations and proofs, that the Sabbath was not then instituted for the first time, but previously known,—the institution known and remembered, but the precise day, perhaps, forgotten during their captivity.

It is agreed on all hands that their journey on the fifteenth was very long. Shaw travelled the same road from Elim. It took his company nine hours from Elim *on Camels* to come to and *cross* the desert of Sin. The Israelites, however, did not go *quite across* it, they stopped in it; but their company consisted of a mixed multitude of men, women, and children, all *on foot*. Therefore, at soonest, they could not have arrived before evening, or six o'clock. Now, let us suppose ourselves present, and watching the time which the various transactions required. Six hundred thousand men, and a proportional number of women and children, arrive at evening. They first pitch their camp; they then examine their stores of provisions; they find them deficient. Then must there have been the working up of a conspiracy, and a communication to and fro among that vast multitude; then the communication from the assembled body to Moses, and from Moses to God; from God to Moses, and from Moses and Aaron to the people. Now what time did all this process require? most certainly not less than twelve hours. In truth, it must have lasted all night. It was then the full of the moon, and any one residing in Ireland knows how favourable moonlight is for works of rebellion. But what time, think you, gentle reader, do Heylyn and Bramhall allow for these transactions? why truly no time at all! the Israelites, according to them, come to the wilderness at even, at six o'clock; and at six o'clock on the same evening, after all these transactions, the quails are sent, and next morning the manna. So that, to make their account possible, time must have stood still during all those transactions.

But what time, think you, gentle reader, was there for all these transactions on Mede's hypothesis? why, truly, much less than no time. He says, that they did not arrive until night. Suppose at nine o'clock; and yet quails came at even, at six o'clock of the same evening. So that to make good his argument, time must not only have stood still, to allow space for those multiplied transactions, but it must have actually gone backwards some hours to get at the even for the coming of the quails. Where now are Bramhall's hours and where is Mede's certainty?

But I have still stronger proof during the progress of the murmuring—take it as early as you please, annihilate time, and place it at even—Moses tells them that in the morning they " shall see the glory of God." And when the glory of the Lord did appear in the morning, the Lord said, " at even ye shall eat flesh, and in the morning ye shall be filled with bread," ver. xvi. 12. "And it came to pass that at even the quails came up, and covered the camp, and in the morning the dew lay round about the host." Now, if the glory which Moses told them they should see in the morning was the glory of the Lord which they really did see in the cloud, the quails were not sent until the evening closing the day after their arrival, nor the manna given until the following morning." The whole of this passage of the Archdeacon's is an attempt to overthrow by a *reductio ad absurdum* the arguments of his opponents founded on their allowing no time or less than none for the accomplishment of a multitude of transactions that could not be accomplished thus instantaneously and while I fully agree their hypothesis as to the manner seems triumphantly overthrown as stated by Mede, Archbishop Bramhall and others, I feel their conclusion not even touched as I shall proceed to shew.

The whole argument of the Archdeacon rests on the supposed length of their journey, and the lateness of their arrival at their halting station and consequently the impossibility of those multiplied transactions which are stated to have happened on that same day, having so happened, namely the forming of a conspiracy the communication between Moses and the people and Moses and God and the sending down of the quails. But in fact the apparent difficulty on the one hand and triumph on the other arises out of unacquaintance with local circumstances as I shall now endeavour to shew 1st by considering the length of the journey 2nd the time of arrival at their halting place and 3rdly I shall test respectively our author's hypothesis and mine by introducing the Scripture narrative of the transactions. 1st relative to the length of the journey it is to be remarked that our author says " though they did not go *quite across* the desert but *stopped in it.* Yet certainly this is not what the sacred record says, Exodus xvi. 1, for here it is distinctly stated that the Children of Israel came UNTO the Wilderness of Sin, now I think that it may be easily allowed that though it took " Shaw with *Camels* nine hours to come to and CROSS the Wilderness of Sin," it might not have taken the Children of Israel even with their mixed multitude *on foot* 4 to have come UNTO it. A man in many situations may come unto the Atlantic in six hours and not come to and CROSS it in six weeks. And that *unto* is the real meaning seems additionally clear from the circumstance that when the glory appeared it was seen TOWARDS the Wilderness, which would have been hardly said, had they been even half way through it, so far then from its being established that they took a very long journey on that day; my full impression is, that they took a very short one in order to rest their cattle and company for the long and difficult march that lay before them in *crossing* the Desert, the constant practice of all caravans. 2ndly, the time of their arrival at their station stated by our author, and his opponents to be about 6 in the evening or 9, appears to me quite inadmissible for either of these hours would necessarily involve the marching through the whole *heat of the day in the month of June* contrary to the universal usage of the country at that season, when the heat of these plains makes the Carnatic appear temperate. It is not surprising that those living in Europe should imagine such a thing, but who would ever think of marching such a multitude of men, women and children, as Moses had under his charge from Madras to Hyderabad in May, from 6 in the morning till 6 at night through the burning heat of the day? The fact is that here lies the whole mistake, the Caravans of Central Asia always begin their march hours before day break even in the Spring and at that period of the year when the Israelites travelled, namely June, soon after midnight in order that they may reach their halting place if it be a short journey (which I believe for the reason I have stated the one of the Israelites on this say to have been) by day light and if it be long about 9 or 10 o'clock. But in the month in which the Israelites took their Journey, namely June, the Caravans from Bagdad to Damascus are 8 weeks in accomplishing a Journey, they at other seasons, accomplish in 4; they rise earlier, particularly when the moon is full, as it was when the journey of the Israelites was performed, and take shorter journies, the order of events therefore appears to me as follows:—

NIGHT MARCH.

The journey commenced on the full of the moon about two or three o'clock in the morning, (according to the constant custom of such Caravans) during this moonlight march, when the passing to and fro among the rebels could not be discerned because of the confusion of the journey the rebellion was ripened, which broke out on their arrival at their halting ground, which appears to have been very early, at day light or before as they appear to have performed this short journey unto the wilderness, in order to have the Cattle fresh and all their encampment up previous to crossing the desert.

ARRIVAL AND BREAKING OUT OF THE REBELLION AT DAY BREAK.

Immediately on their arrival and the breaking out of the rebellion messages passed between Moses and the people, and Moses and God, and while Aaron was making his last communication from Moses to the people the glory of the Lord appeared and promised in the evening quails and on the morning manna.

IN THE EVENING OF THE 16TH QUAILS CAME.

In the morning of the 16th, Manna was given, the days commencing at 6 in the evening, and terminating at 6 in the next evening.

3rdly. I here subjoin the Scripture account that my readers may judge for themselves as to which account adheres closest to scripture. And they took their journey from Elim, and all the congregation of the Children of

Israel came *unto* the wilderness of Sin, which is between Elim and Sinai, on the fifteenth *day* of the second month after their departing out of the land of Egypt. And the whole congregation of the Children of Israel murmured against Moses and Aaron in the wilderness. And the Children of Israel said unto them, would to God we had died by the hand of the Lord in the land of Egypt, when we sat by the flesh pots, and when we did eat bread to the full; for ye have brought us forth into this wilderness, to kill this whole assembly with hunger. Then said the Lord unto Moses, Behold I will rain bread from heaven for you; and the people shall go out and gather a certain rate every day, that I may prove them whether they will walk in my law, or no. And it shall come to pass that on the 6th day they shall prepare that which they bring in; and it shall be twice as much as they gather daily; and Moses and Aaron said unto all the children of Israel, at even then ye shall know that the Lord hath brought you out from the land of Egypt: And in the morning, then ye shall see the glory of the Lord; and what are we, that ye murmur against us? And Moses said, this shall be when the Lord shall give you in the evening flesh to eat, and in the morning bread to the full; for that the Lord heareth your murmurings which ye murmur against him: and what are we? your murmurings are not against us, but against the Lord. And Moses spake unto Aaron; say unto all the congregation of the children of Israel, come near before the Lord: for he hath heard your murmurings. And it came to pass as Aaron spake unto the whole congregation of the children of Israel, that they looked towards the wilderness, and behold the glory of the Lord appeared in the cloud and the Lord spake unto Moses saying, I have heard the murmurings of the children of Israel, speak unto them saying. At even ye shall eat flesh, and in the morning ye shall be filled with bread, and ye shall know that I am the Lord your God. And it came to pass that at even the quails came up, and covered the camp, and in the morning the dew lay round about the host. In the above quotation there is not a shadow of ground for supposing they arrived at *even* but the contrary it is said they arrived on the 15th *day* and when Moses tells them there shall be flesh in the even given them he does not say to-morrow even but speaks just as one would who had arrived at his station in the morning early when alluding to an event that was to happen that same evening neither does there appear any break in the narrative from the breaking out of the conspiracy to the appearing of the glory but while Aaron was giving Moses's reply to the conspirators the glory appeared. I have dwelt at some length on this point because it exhibits a fair specimen of the kind of refutation with which this volume abounds on many similar points and to shew how deceptive such may be and also because by two or three times referring to what the Archdeacon considers a *demonstrative* overthrow of the opinions of his opponents he shews he had great complacency in contemplating the achievement he had performed and I think there is no one who has read the Archbishops little publication but must feel that the spirit in which the enquiry is carried on by him at all events might have been with great profit followed by the Archdeacon much more closely than it has.

Appendix C.

There is another argument appended to the above which is the objection our author has to suppose that so illogical a mode of stating the 4th and 5th verses of the xvi. ch: should have been allowed that is telling men about the manna without defining why the sixth day was to have a double quantity, unless they had previously known why it was, yet surely that Scripture to which the Archdeacon's professes so closely to adhere shews they did not know, for what did they do when they had gathered the double portion on the 6th day. Did they act as men who knew what they were to do with it or what it was for? not at all but when on the 6th day they had gathered twice as much the rulers came to Moses and told him; and then he explained to them in the following words the reason of it and he said (Ex. xvi. 22, 23). And it came to pass that on the sixth day they gathered twice as much bread two omers for one man: and all the rulers of the congregation came and told Moses and he said unto them this is the thing which the Lord hath said to-morrow is the rest of the holy sabbath unto the Lord: bake that which ye will bake, and seethe that which ye will seethe; and that which remaineth over lay up for you to be kept until the morning. The impression the unprejudiced reading of these two verses seem calculated to make on any mind, both from the ignorance of the people and the answer of Moses is that the institution as far as it related to *rest* was new; and the whole passage to the 30th verse, Moses telling them in the 25th verse this is a sabbath, and many of them going out to gather manna as well as another to gather sticks and Moses' ignorance what to do with him shews that all rules relative to its observance were new to all.

ERRATA.

Page   5 note   *for*   Angels   *read*   Angles.
—— 30 line 16 —   and   —   I.
—— 32 note 22 —   new mode —   use made.
—— 68 line 24 the Greek is upside down.
—— 100 3d last line *read* (see Appendix A) after the words, But really rest.
—— 112 line 15 *for* Apostalise *read* Apostatise.
—— 117 — 1 —   or   —   as.
—— —— —— 6 —   judically, —   judicially.

www.ingramcontent.com/pod-product-compliance
Lightning Source LLC
LaVergne TN
LVHW061216060426
835507LV00016B/1953